The Spokesman

Obama's Afghan Dilemma

Edited by Ken Coates

Published by Spokesman for the
Bertrand Russell Peace Foundation

Spokesman 99　　　　　　　　　　　　　**2008**

CONTENTS

Cover: *With thanks to Steve Bell.*
Printed by the Russell Press Ltd., Nottingham, UK
ISSN 1367 7748
ISBN 978 0 85124 753 3

Subscriptions
Institutions £35.00
Individuals £20.00 (UK)
　　　　　£25.00 (ex UK)

Back issues available on
request

A CIP catalogue record
for this book is available
from the British Library

Published by the
Bertrand Russell Peace
Foundation Ltd.,
Russell House
Bulwell Lane
Nottingham NG6 0BT
England
Tel. 0115 9784504
email:
elfeuro@compuserve.com
www.spokesmanbooks.com
www.russfound.org

Editorial

Ending the War without End
Obama's Afghan Dilemma

I
Taking stock of Afghan wars

When asked for his motto, Karl Marx said 'doubt everything'. Never was this better advice than in the case of official views about the war in Iraq. Even more is this true in the case of hostilities in Afghanistan.

What is not in doubt is that the cost of operations in Afghanistan continues to mount, and the casualties relentlessly levy their toll. More dubious are the apologies for this war. A whole group of the critics of the war in Iraq have sought a bolthole from the reproach that they have lacked patriotic ardour by aggressively arguing that too much mayhem in Iraq has made more difficult what they now claim to be the more necessary war in Afghanistan. Notable among these people is, apparently, Barack Obama, whose views we must consider later.[1]

Initially, the conflict between the United States and the Taliban Government was directed towards the destruction of Al Qaeda, and the Taliban were led to think that maybe they could be spared if they gave up Osama Bin Laden and surrendered his men for punishment. Hostilities were not, in the beginning, mainly pursued by American boots on the ground, but by extensive bribery and the deployment of remorseless air power. The bribery was shrewdly directed towards the warlords along the northern border of the country. Some of these people, but by no means all, were simply bandits and the operation depended on the passive engagement and air bases of Central Asian Republics from the former Soviet Union. At that time the Russians looked kindly on the American War on Terror, although their ardour may have been somewhat cooled by subsequent United States depredations and subversions in the territories of the 'near abroad'. Thus, some of America's cash-conscious Afghan allies became a wasting asset, and it is a little early to evaluate the significance of renewed agreements on the use of the airbase in Uzbekistan.[2]

As the post 9/11 Afghan war opened up, United States special operations provided a few hundred soldiers, along with a number of CIA operatives who were more or less familiar with the terrain, having previously nurtured and then sustained the forces of Osama Bin Laden. A vast resource in air power was the most material help given to the formerly Russian and Iranian sponsored warlord forces who finally lanced the Taliban boil. But they did this by relying on their ability to call down American air strikes which were most effective against the cities. This rather firmly persuaded the Taliban to withdraw from cities and targetable emplacements and repair to the countryside.

We are reminded of the story of Brer Rabbit, who was captured by Brer Fox, and threatened with brutal punishment. 'Do not' said Brer Rabbit, 'whatever you do, put me into the briar patch, Brer Fox. Anything but the briar patch.' Not unnaturally, Brer Fox, like the Americans, immediately threw Brer Rabbit, just like the Taliban, into the briar patch. 'Born and bred in the briar patch', said the Taliban, as they withdrew and readied themselves for a renaissance.

In the event, Al Qaeda was disrupted but not destroyed. American military deployment did much to revive and extend it. The Taliban, in contrast, maintained much if not most of their military capacity. The newly elected Government of Afghanistan, headed by Hamid Karzai, was advertised as expected to defeat the Taliban in due course, and it was to help it that 50,000 troops were subsequently despatched by various Nato members to Afghanistan. Unfortunately, these proved inadequate to contain the Taliban forces, while the Americans themselves deployed enough soldiers to hold major cities and, from time to time, mount forays which could hinder the Taliban in the countryside, whilst widely alienating the surrounding population.

In their previous Afghan war, the Russians had been defeated, having deployed 300,000 troops. The Russians also sponsored a number of social policies which won them a degree of actual support in Afghan cities, so that it would be interesting to know how the attendance of girls in schools compares then with now. The combined forces of Nato today muster one-sixth of the numbers engaged in the Soviet forces, but they are likely to be less effective. Their Commanders have scrabbled and bickered all around Afghanistan, and the much-vaunted solidarity of that beleaguered alliance has been severely tested. Some have lined up for combatant duties, providing at the same time a photogenic role for junior members of the British Royal Household. Others appear to have volunteered mainly for parading or other forms of display. Acrimony between the different camps knows no bounds, and the Canadians have announced that they will be off out of it if their allies do not shoulder greater burdens. All the while, the Taliban insurgency has been improving its range and performance. Across the border, in Pakistan, severe doubts arise about the commitment of Mr. Musharraf's allied forces, and even about the President's survival, whilst Taliban sympathisers range widely across his country. To be fair, it is pretty clear that from the beginning the Americans had no desire to reconstruct, or do anything very much, with Afghanistan. They needed to protect the Karzai Government, which has been universally described as the local government of Kabul. This was necessary to confer legitimacy on the foreign forces which sustained it, and to counter Al Qaeda, supposed to be holed up in Pakistan, perhaps more than to hamper the Taliban's efforts in Afghanistan. But it was seen for what it was: an outpost, an imperial token, rather than an effective alternative to the rural anarchy which the Americans, like all their predecessors, had decided was, in principle, completely ungovernable.

So what are all those troops engaged to do? They cannot modify the real situation on the ground in Afghanistan. If they don't try, they won't be disappointed, and modern Generals tend to avoid disappointment wherever possible. It has been argued that Afghanistan found a role for Nato, to maintain its cohesion. That cohesion is perhaps more doubtful now than it was before so many foreigners voyaged to Central Asia.

II
Opium wars

The first excuse for renewing the offensive in Afghanistan is that it is necessary to put an end to the opium trade. After the overthrow of the Taliban, this grew by leaps and bounds under the protection of the victorious warlords. Previously, it had been outlawed by the Taliban from the year 2000. Before that, three-quarters of the opium poppies in the world grew in Afghanistan, but a decree of July 27th 2000 forbade their cultivation. This took instant effect, and from 12,600 acres at the time of its promulgation, the area under poppies shrank to seventeen within six months. No poppies were allowed under the Taliban.

The warlords, however, put paid to that regime. Free enterprise has seen opium flourish, from 75 per cent of world production before the Taliban decree, to 87 per cent in 2005, and 90 per cent in 2006. In the heady days of Empire, Queen Victoria's brave men could tackle this problem by launching a full-scale war on China to persuade the Chinese to abrogate their prohibition of the drug, and re-open the market. Today, the Chinese might prove unreasonably obdurate on this matter.

It has been suggested that the production of opium might cease to be a problem if it were all sold to approved customers among the allies. How many poppies could the National Health Services usefully use? Until now, this welfare solution for the farmers of Helmand has not gathered influential support among the Governments whose forces are embattled there. Opium output grows remorselessly, but the American experiments with lethal sprays have to be applied extremely judiciously for fear of antagonising Afghan hearts and minds.

The extinction of the Taliban is an even more elusive goal than is the uprooting of all those poppies. The insurgents continue to prosper, and the longer they do so, the less likely are the Nato allies to prevail. Michael McConnell, the Director of National Intelligence in the USA, reported at the end of February 2008 that President Karzai's forces control less than one-third of the country, while the Taliban holds sway over ten or eleven per cent of it. The rest is held locally, often by warlords. The undoubted resilience of Taliban forces stems at least in part from the fact that they are fighting in their own country, and they do not know where else to go. But their occupiers may well be thanking their lucky stars that Afghanistan is not their own country, and looking forward quite avidly to the prospect of going home. British soldiers used to have an anthem which accurately expressed their view of such matters: 'we're here because we're here because we're here', they sang.

III
What do you get for your money when you buy warlords?

Meantime, not only body bags, but bills continue to arrive to the distress of all the allies. The bills of the Americans have now become acutely difficult to sustain. Joseph Stiglitz, the Nobel Prize winning economist, has completed a painstaking enquiry into the cost of the wars in Iraq and Afghanistan.[3] At the moment, these run to $16 billion for the Americans alone every month, over and above their regular defence expenditure. The cumulative cost, to America alone, is $3 trillion.

Needless to say this staggering sum was not imagined anywhere at the time that hostilities commenced.

At the beginning, one could buy a substantial phalanx of warlords for a pittance, and the CIA normally disposed of a good deal more than a pittance. The heavy ordinance that could be called in for air raids was expensive, but it had been stored up for precisely such an eventuality as this. The British commitments added a considerable volume of rhetoric, and what passes for moral support.

One of the warlords in Afghanistan who might have been able to demand something more than a pittance from the American dispensers of funds was Abdul Rashid Dostum, who probably still holds the title of General, and Chief of Staff to the Commander in Chief of the Afghan National Army. Not all of his forces believe that this title reflects reality. Many of his supporters regard it as more than a little honorific. What is certainly true, however, is that he is recognised as a main leader of the Uzbek community in Afghanistan.

His career has been somewhat colourful, and he has participated, on various

---

Where is all the money going?

As I sit here in Afghanistan on my third 'Combat' deployment, I ask myself one question; where is all of the money going? I did a combat deployment at the beginning of 2003 on the USS *Theodore Roosevelt* at the start of Operation Iraqi Freedom for 'Shock and Awe'. I watched the planes I worked on take off the pointy end of the ship armed to the teeth with Mavericks, JDAMs, GBUs, AMRAAMs, Sparrows, HARMS, and Sidewinders to take out strategic targets as well as provide close air support in Northern Iraq for the 101st Airborne, and the 173rd Armored Brigade. It was pretty amazing, granted at the time I supported the war in Iraq, due to ignorance on my part. For the summer of 2006, I sat in Al Asad, Iraq, and I watched the planes I currently work on, take off into the desert sky, and support the troop convoys all over the roads in Central Iraq by tactically jamming improvised explosive device signals. Now, currently, I watch those same planes take off into the frozen Afghani night sky to do a 'new' mission, one that has yet to be unclassified. Being in the Naval Aviation, you expect to do your deployments on an Aircraft Carrier, not as a 'Dirt Sailor', but who cares, I'm here, trying to do my job the best I can. Back to my point, where's all the money going? In October 2001, the President said something along the lines of 'We're gonna get the guy who did this (bin Laden)'. Well, he was in Afghanistan, and apparently we weren't fast enough, and he got away, so we needed a new war to 'win'. So we invaded Iraq, under false pretences, and have yet to 'win' that one. If Osama bin Laden is such a bad motherfucker, why do we only have 27,000 troops in Afghanistan looking for him, and 130,000+ troops in Iraq staving off a civil war? Living arrangements on a ship are living arrangements on a ship, they don't change from ship to ship, it is the same damn 'coffin'. Ship life is ship life, it never changes, Groundhog Day takes on a new meaning when you are floating for 6 months. In Iraq, I had it pretty sweet compared to boat life. In each 'can', there were two sailors, furniture, an air conditioner (a must, it was 125 every day), and huge concrete barriers sides, in almost all of the myriad conflicts which have torn his country asunder. Since 1970, when he got a job in the nationalised gas refinery in Sheberghan, he has served in a variety of military forces. He joined up with the Afghan army in 1978, and fought the Mujahideen throughout the next decade. In 1992 he joined forces with Ahmad Shah Masoud of the Northern Alliance, to fight against Gulbuddin Hekmatyar. In 1996 the Taliban took Kabul, so that Dostum was driven in retreat to Mazar-i-Sharif.

The following year his lieutenant, General Abdul Malik, defected to the Taliban, and Dostum withdrew from the battle to seek refuge in Turkey. Soon afterwards Malik changed his allegiances again, and was able to hand over thousands of Taliban, including many juveniles, to their enemies, who slaughtered between six and eight thousand of them. The Taliban rallied and subjugated Malik's group, and he took refuge in Washington before withdrawing to Iran.

Dostum, for his part, waited for the call, and in April 2001, it came when Massoud invited him to open up a Western front against the Taliban. So it was that

---

around our camp to protect us from indirect fire (which we received often). Our BX/PX was like a damn Wal-Mart, aisle upon aisle of EVERYTHING you could possibly need in a combat OR to live a tolerable life. Our hangar was a huge Hardened Aircraft Shelter, a relic of the Saddam Era, but a good facility nonetheless. We had to team up with the Seabees to build it up to our standards, but we were provided everything we needed in minimal time. Here in Afghanistan, it is quite a different story. My living quarters are pathetic. It's a particleboard hut, with seven other dudes, some of us only separated by sheets. No room is the same, and we have only two heaters per hut (that aren't always working). Oh yeah, it has yet to get above 40 degrees F since I've been here. These particleboard houses have been fire tested by the Army, and the average time for one to be FULLY engulfed in flames is 3 minutes, 30 seconds. Rather unsettling considering mine is 45 feet from the perimeter fence. Our BX/PX is 'sufficient' at best. It has a bare minimum of stuff you don't need, and they sell the same crap they give away at the DFAC, wtf? Our 'hangar' if you can call it that, is like a big circus tent. They call it a 'clamshell', probably because it opens like a clam, but it is the stupidest thing ever. If it were to take a direct hit from an rocket propelled grenade it would melt in no time flat. EVERYTHING on this base in Afghanistan is either made out of plywood, or old shipping containers. Everything in Iraq was all nice and either brand new or refurbished. If Osama is such a bad motherfucker, and we want his head, why don't we pour some money into Afghanistan instead of into Iraq? Why don't we utilize the greatest fighting force on the planet to catch guys who are actually the 'bad guys', instead of using them for the benefit of a small group of people and their personal interests? If you ask me, the priorities in this region are all fucked up, and something needs to change.

AME1(AW) James S. Huetteman
US Navy, Deployed.
15 February 2008, posted on www.ivaw.org

he found himself embattled alongside the American invading forces in spite of the fact that the CIA nourished considerable distrust for him. The American forces were led by Mike Spann, the first casualty from the United States to be killed in that war, alongside one hundred and twenty Afghans and most of the foreign forces who accompanied him.

In November 2002 unnamed witnesses told Jamie Doran, a former BBC television producer, the story of some thousands of Taliban prisoners who surrendered to Dostum's forces after the siege of Kunduz (see *Spokesman 77*). Three thousand of the prisoners were forced into sealed containers and loaded on to trucks, allegedly for transport to the prison at Sheberghan. Suffocating, the prisoners began to cry out for air. Dostum's soldiers fired into the trucks, killing many of those inside them. The rest underwent a long slow trek by road, without water and deprived of fresh air. The death toll was horrific. Doran's film was contested by witnesses who claimed that it was untrue.

Dostum established a Northern zone of Afghanistan, against the wishes of Hamid Karzai, now the interim President. It was after that, on May 20th 2003, that he assumed the title of Chief of Staff to the Commander in Chief of the Afghan Armed Forces. Armed conflict soon broke out in the North, between Dostum and the Tajik General Ustad Atta Mohammed Noor. This required intensive efforts by the American led coalition and the Nato forces to establish an uneasy and truculent *modus vivendi*.

On February 2nd 2008, some fifty members of the Dostum forces attacked the home of Akbar Bai, who had challenged the rule of the General. Bai was beaten up and taken prisoner, as was his son and a bodyguard. He was liberated by Afghan police who arrested Dostum, surrounding his house. The Afghan Attorney General sought to bring charges against Dostum, accusing him of kidnapping, assault, and breaking and entering.

From his hospital bed, where he has been nursed for 'serious injuries', Mr. Bai has levelled a formal complaint that the General 'has committed a crime and must be punished if there is law and democracy in this country. This is on top of many other crimes he has committed'.

Attorney General Abdul Jabar Sabat was reported as saying that:

> 'The case is that someone enters someone else's house in the middle of Kabul city 500 metres from the presidential palace, beats the people in that house, kidnaps them and abuses them. If the law is not implemented against such a person, it means there is no law at all. If General Dostum knew there was the certainty of the law being implemented, he would not dare to have done it.'[4]

General Dostum is reported as having retired to his base at Sheberghan in the North. His retainers are being rearmed, and his supporters hold daily demonstrations threatening an uprising if the arrest warrant against him is not revoked and if his official powers are not restored. Nato's Northern forces may need more than their diplomatic skills to sort out the problems which are maturing at Sheberghan.

IV
First time tragedy, second time farce:
Britain goes East of Suez again

The United Kingdom styled its intervention in Afghanistan as Operation Veritas, which had four objectives: to deny Al Qaeda its base in Afghanistan; to deny them any alternative bases; to attack them internationally; and to support others who were pursuing similar efforts.

It was in October 2001 that the Americans launched Operation Enduring Freedom, with the British in support. Submarines from the Royal Navy fired Tomahawk missiles at targets which they assured us included Taliban and Al Qaeda capabilities. The RAF reconnoitred in support of such targeting, and provided refuelling capacities to American strike aircraft. Diego Garcia, the 'British' island leased out to the Americans as a deniable base, flew as many missions as were necessary, while others dropped down from Uzbekistan and adjacent territories. British troops finally arrived in Afghanistan to secure the airfield at Bagram in November 2001. One thousand seven hundred British Marines continued to be deployed after this operation, destroying bunkers and caves, and offering humanitarian assistance to villages which had formerly been under the control of the Taliban. This commitment came to an end in July 2002.

After December 2001, the United Nations Security Council Resolution 1386 mobilised sixteen member-states into a military mission to secure the Afghan Transitional Authority in Kabul and police its surrounding neighbourhoods. Britain contributed the brigade headquarters and a battalion of infantrymen. 'Our contribution initially peaked at 2,100 troops, later decreasing to around three hundred personnel after the transfer of the leadership of the UN forces to Turkey in the summer of 2002.'[5] The mission of these UN forces, including the British, was to train non-commissioned officers for the Afghan National Army. The British also set up a 'Sandhurst' style amenity in Kabul, and operational liaison teams in Helmand.

In 2003, Nato took over the responsibilities that had previously been discharged by the United Nations under Security Council Resolution 1510. The Rapid Reaction Force under these auspices engaged about a thousand British troops. The following year six Harrier jets were deployed to Kandahar to help these forces. Staged Nato expansion, aimed at 'extending the writ of the Kabul Government', began during the presidential elections of October 2004.

By the end of July 2006 the third of these stages was entered, taking the Nato forces into Southern Afghanistan, where eight member-states are contributing some ten thousand troops. The main forces come from the UK, the United States, Canada and The Netherlands, with additional support from Denmark, Estonia, Australia and Romania.

A fourth stage of this expansion, in October 2006, extended the reach of the UN forces' deployment over the whole territory of Afghanistan for the first time. It also sharpened the conflict between different members of Nato, who were deployed under different regimes of engagement, reflecting their national jurisdictions and specific rules of engagement. The expenditure entailed in these deployments is not inconsiderable. But the tally of American costs is evidently much larger. This is augmented by the propensity of American funds to evaporate, or 'fall between the cracks at the Department of Defence'. For ten years now this has resoundingly defeated the official auditors, who have been unable to approve a single annual audit. There was a famous case in which $8.8 billion of development funding, the responsibility of the Coalition Provisional Authority in Iraq, simply went absent without leave. It has never been recovered. The principles of free enterprise have been widely applied in occupied Iraq to say nothing of Afghanistan, and nowhere more evidently than among the occupiers themselves.

British rules might be more stringent. Certainly they used to be. Denis Healey, reporting on his efforts to annul military commitments East of Suez, describes a grand tour which he made of the principal assets in the Gulf States. One famous dignitary, let him be discreetly veiled as the Akond of Swat, generously decorated all Healey's advisory team with elegant wristwatches, reserving for their leader a magnificent gold Rolex of great solidity and weight. Upon returning home, the appropriate Civil Service gauleiters examined all this booty, and graciously announced that all the small fry could keep their modest watches, but that the Minister must surrender his indecently large gold bauble to the State. Healey ruefully reports in his Memoirs that the next time that he saw this precious object was in the Cabinet Room, where it was gracing the wrist of Harold Wilson. But we must suppose that it is the thought that counts.

Be that as it may, a substantial proportion of the American budgetary effort must be accounted for in various forms of corruption, which is not likely to be so true of British expenditure. There is, of course, corruption and corruption. A mercenary employed as a security guard in Iraq is paid $400,000 a year: while an ordinary American soldier is estimated to receive about $40,000. Perhaps matters are made worse by the fact that the American Government steps into the breach vacated by insurance companies, to cover its mercenaries, and to pay death and injury benefits over and above that cover. A kind of Gresham's law takes effect, ensuring that recruits are very hard to find for the American army, since any with lingering ambitions in that direction would be foolish to avoid the lure of the mercenaries, thus marrying the call of patriotism to that of free market propriety.

Stiglitz's calculations have explored these niceties, and persuaded him that the minimum cost of America's wars in these theatres has run at $2 trillion, while the more likely actual cost has run at $3 trillion. The cost for all the other allies and partners in the various coalitions is estimated at as much again, but obviously this is only a guess. What is not a guess is Stiglitz's computation of the alternative uses of even $1 trillion worth of expenditure: health care for 530 million children, or the construction of eight million houses.

Aid for Africa has recently been a fashionable cause. The Americans are spending $5 billion a year on this cause, or, as Stiglitz points out, roughly ten days fighting, 'so you get a new metric of thinking about everything'.

For how long can this insane activity be continued? None of this military waste has been funded by direct taxation. All bills were paid by borrowing. The patrimony of future generations, even in the remarkable economy of the United States, will thus ensure a continuing bondage of debt down the ages. Who can take the pen and cross off these mighty obligations? How can wars of these dimensions be written off? The dead, both combatant, and non-combatant victims, are a standing and continuing reproach to all of us. But age will in fact wither memories, and States will forget those heroes. However, the debts are a reproach that will not be allowed to go away while the rule of money, raw red in tooth and claw, continues to hold its terroristic sway.

The rules of financial prudence, alas, do not normally apply to wars. Once the bloodlust is on them, statesmen lose any knowledge they may once have had of the laws of arithmetic. A paradigm case of this forgetfulness can be found in the British Government, parsimonious in the extreme when it concerns elderly pensioners or juvenile tots.

Currently the British Royal Navy is mired in a severe dilemma about procurement. Conservative Governments had been cutting the resources for the Navy as long ago as 1982, and this was the subject of considerable debate during the early days of the Falklands War. Cutbacks were arrested, but resumed when the war was safely over and the Cold War was in its declining years. Major cuts took place from 1991, and warships are now being retired quite remorselessly, even though their replacement has been intermittent and sluggish. The result is that a surge in procurement is on the cards, slumps and evil economic weather probably notwithstanding.

The biggest ships involved are two aircraft carriers, the bare shells of which are expected to cost £3.6 billion, without allowing for the planes they are supposed to deploy, which will be purchased, no doubt at a considerable price, from the United States. They will be F-35 Lightning Two Joint Strike Fighters. An alliance like this one must be deemed a considerable asset, at any rate for someone. Ranged behind the carriers is the nuclear-powered attack submarine, already £1 billion over budget, and four years behind schedule. Then there is the Type 45 Daring Guided Missile Destroyer programme, the leading ship of which will cost £1 billion, and the programme for which is already £1 billion over budget and two and a half years behind schedule.

What are all these attack forces for? Against whom are they directed? Long ago, when Denis Healey was sent a-voyaging, a British Labour Government ended its commitment to police the world East of Suez. Then it was allegedly being policed in the British interest, although careful assessments revealed that the Empire was costing more than it was yielding in dividends. But today's Empire does not belong to the British, and does not pay any dividends to the British Exchequer.

Hard-pressed social services need the new East of Suez policy like they need a hole in the head. In fact, they will be very lucky if a hole in the head is all they get from this lunatic commitment.

Some of this Naval rubbish will undoubtedly be acquired. But since cuts will be inevitable, it will all cost over the odds. The economies of scale, which reduce the costs of the second and subsequent units progressively, will not be available. All these loud announcements about the impending modernisation of Naval forces are supposed to indicate a degree of Governmental priority. Unfortunately, there is no priority whatever for rational analysis of foreign policy objectives or even of the costs and benefits of military decisions.

The Afghan chaos is currently in danger of spilling into Pakistan. Already the forces of the Taliban operate across the frontier of the two countries to their considerable advantage. American Generals regret this fact, and show themselves quite open to the idea that frontiers are imaginary lines. It is not only Generals who think like this. This understanding impacted on South Waziristan in March 2008 when "'three bombs ... dropped by American aircraft killed nine people and wounded nine others," a Pakistani security official said'. This was the third raid on Pakistan in less than three months.[6]

We feature below an important declaration on foreign policy by Senator Barack Obama, which ought to ring alarm bells in London. The alarm bells already rang at the beginning of March 2008, with the resignation of Admiral William J. Fallon, Commander of Centcom, the American Central Command. Informed commentators tell us that this resignation was either a protest, or a dismissal. In what respect was Fallon deemed to have failed? He cannot easily be accused of failure, when the regime in Washington is trumpeting the success of the recent surge in Iraq.

We have documented some part of the astonishing shambles in Afghanistan, which is ripening into a grisly farce. Undoubtedly that shambles is underpinned and reinforced by the Pakistan dimension. Just as the insurgence rolls back and forth across the frontier, so its consequences destabilise what passes for political authority in Pakistan itself.

This is the context in which a military surge is being proposed for the American forces in Afghanistan. If such a surge does go where the action appears to take it, randomly traversing the boundaries, a sinister dimension affects Gordon Brown's new East of Suez policy. For him, Pakistan is not simply a distant country, with exotic customs. He has got Pakistan at home, as well. East of Suez can all too easily mean mayhem in the Home Counties.

V
USA: New deal or no deal?

Barack Obama has aroused much admiration among a new generation of Americans, to say nothing of his influence abroad. He is perceived by many as an anti-establishment figure, and nobody likes the American Establishment. His criticism of the war in Iraq has won him many friends. But the Afghan turmoil is no more worthy of support than is the bloodbath in Iraq. It is not going anywhere, and even if it were, it would encompass many wrongs. How can we account for Obama's apparent ambivalence? Does he believe that the Taliban bore direct responsibility for 9/11? This is a doubtful proposition, since Al Qaeda had its own chains of influence and command. But even if it were true, how would condign punishment of Afghan peasants redress the undoubted wrongs inflicted in New York?

Barack Obama numbers among his foreign policy advisors none other than

Zbigniew Brzezinski, to whom we have made reference before. His version of geopolitical realities has chilled us to the marrow more than once. How far has he fixed his claws into this young hopeful, who might yet be President?

We should surely recall Brzezinski's interview with *Le Nouvel Observateur* (Jan 15-21, 1998):

'**Q:** The former director of the CIA, Robert Gates, stated in his memoirs ['From the Shadows'], that American intelligence services began to aid the Mujahideen in Afghanistan six months before the Soviet intervention. In this period you were the national security adviser to President Carter. You therefore played a role in this affair. Is that correct?

Brzezinski: Yes. According to the official version of history, CIA aid to the Mujahideen began during 1980, that is to say, after the Soviet army invaded Afghanistan, 24 Dec 1979. But the reality, secretly guarded until now, is completely otherwise. Indeed, it was July 3, 1979 that President Carter signed the first directive for secret aid to the opponents of the pro-Soviet regime in Kabul. And that very day, I wrote a note to the President in which I explained to him that in my opinion this aid was going to induce a Soviet military intervention.

Q: Despite this risk, you were an advocate of this covert action. But perhaps you yourself desired this Soviet entry into war and looked to provoke it?

Brzezinski: It isn't quite that. We didn't push the Russians to intervene, but we knowingly increased the probability that they would.

Q: When the Soviets justified their intervention by asserting that they intended to fight against a secret involvement of the United States in Afghanistan, people didn't believe them. However, there was a basis of truth. You don't regret anything today?

Brzezinski: Regret what? That secret operation was an excellent idea. It had the effect of drawing the Russians into the Afghan trap and you want me to regret it? The day that the Soviets officially crossed the border, I wrote to President Carter: we now have the opportunity of giving to the USSR its Vietnam war. Indeed, for almost 10 years, Moscow had to carry on a war unsupportable by the government, a conflict that brought about the demoralization and finally the break-up of the Soviet empire.[7]

Q: And neither do you regret having supported the Islamic [integrisme], having given arms and advice to future terrorists?

Brzezinski: What is most important to the history of the world? The Taliban or the collapse of the Soviet empire? Some stirred-up Moslems or the liberation of Central Europe and the end of the Cold War?

Q: Some stirred-up Moslems? But it has been said and repeated: Islamic fundamentalism represents a world menace today.

Brzezinski: Nonsense! It is said that the West had a global policy in regard to Islam. That is stupid. There isn't a global Islam. Look at Islam in a rational manner and without demagoguery or emotion. It is the leading religion of the world with 1.5 billion followers. But what is there in common among Saudi Arabian fundamentalism, moderate Morocco, Pakistan militarism, Egyptian pro-Western or Central Asian secularism? Nothing more than what unites the Christian countries.'

We may not be alone in suggesting that the advice of Zbigniew Brzezinski comes from a poisoned chalice. Those who can influence the new President might be well-advised to proceed with caution. As he candidly admits, Zbig is not much interested in the fate of Afghanistan itself, but he is likely to be an assiduous promoter of the Second Cold War, already vigorously maturing with the enlargement of Nato and related policies of nuclear deployment around Russia. Why is he so very critical of the Iraq war? Could it be that he fears America is losing sight of his main enemy?

Ken Coates

Notes

1 See below, pages 15 to 25.

2 Karshi-Khanabad airbase is among the biggest in the former Soviet Union, and serviced the Soviet forces during their Afghan war from 1979-1989. The Americans leased this facility for similar purposes during its main offensive against the Taliban. But quarrels about the lamentable human rights record of the Uzbek Government, and fears of the surge of American-backed Rose and Orange revolutions, persuaded the Uzbek Government to throw out the American forces in 2005. If it is true that Nato is about to be allowed back into Karshi-Khanabad, we may expect a boost to the hyperactivity of Nato forces. This is likely to give rise to fractious responses among the less fanatical of America's allies.

3 Joseph Stiglitz and Linda Bilmes: *The Three Trillion Dollar War*, Allen Lane, £20.

4 *The Independent*, 11 March 2008.

5 Ministry of Defence Factsheet, 'Operations in Afghanistan: Background Briefing 1 – The background to UK military involvement in Afghanistan'.

6 *New York Times*, 17 March 2008.

7 A new memoir on the work of the CIA, by a sometime official, Frank Wisner, recalls the young Brzezinski's appearance as a disrupter of the Vienna Youth Festival in 1959: 'Having sneaked into the Soviet encampment, Zbigniew Brzezinski (the son of a Polish diplomat) walked openly among its Russian residents deliberately bumping into them and saying in Russian, with a heavy Polish accent, "Out of my way, Russian pig!" in a deliberate attempt to stir ill-feeling between the Russian and Polish contingents.' The CIA's techniques became more sophisticated, but Mr Brzezinski apparently retains his antipathy for 'Russian pigs', even if, today, they are more likely to be 'capitalist pigs', than communist ones. Source: Hugh Wilford, *The Mighty Wurlitzer: How the CIA Played America*, pp145-146, Harvard University Press.

Afghan Dilemma

Barack Obama

Senator Obama gave this speech at the Woodrow Wilson Center for International Scholars in Washington DC on 1 August 2007. He was introduced by Lee H. Hamilton, President and Director of the Center.

Thank you Lee, for hosting me here at the Wilson Center, and for your leadership of both the 9/11 Commission and the Iraq Study Group. You have been a steady voice of reason in an unsteady time.

Let me also say that my thoughts and prayers are with your colleague, Haleh Esfandiari, and her family. I have made my position known to the Iranian government. It is time for Haleh to be released. It is time for Haleh to come home.

Thanks to the 9/11 Commission, we know that six years ago this week President Bush received a briefing with the headline: 'Bin Ladin determined to strike in US'. It came during what the Commission called the 'summer of threat', when the 'system was blinking red' about an impending attack. But despite the briefing, many felt the danger was overseas, a threat to embassies and military installations. The extremism, the resentment, the terrorist training camps, and the killers were in the dark corners of the world, far away from the American homeland.

Then, one bright and beautiful Tuesday morning, they were here.

I was driving to a state legislative hearing in downtown Chicago when I heard the news on my car radio: a plane had hit the World Trade Center. By the time I got to my meeting, the second plane had hit, and we were told to evacuate.

People gathered in the streets and looked up at the sky and the Sears Tower, transformed from a workplace to a target. We feared for our families and our country. We mourned the terrible loss suffered by our fellow citizens. Back at my law office, I watched the images from New York: a plane vanishing into glass and steel; men and women clinging to windowsills, then letting go; tall towers crumbling to dust. It seemed all of the misery and all of the evil in the world were in that rolling black cloud, blocking out the September sun.

What we saw that morning forced us to recognize that in a new world of threats, we are no longer protected by our own power. And what we saw that morning was a challenge to a new generation.

The history of America is one of tragedy turned into triumph. And so a war over secession became an opportunity to set the captives free. An attack on Pearl Harbor led to a wave of freedom rolling across the Atlantic and Pacific. An Iron Curtain was punctured by democratic values, new institutions at home, and strong international partnerships abroad.

After 9/11, our calling was to write a new chapter in the American story. To devise new strategies and build new alliances, to secure our homeland and safeguard our values, and to serve a just cause abroad. We were ready. Americans were united. Friends around the world stood shoulder to shoulder with us. We had the might and moral-suasion that was the legacy of generations of Americans. The tide of history seemed poised to turn, once again, toward hope.

But then everything changed.

We did not finish the job against Al Qaeda in Afghanistan. We did not develop new capabilities to defeat a new enemy, or launch a comprehensive strategy to dry up the terrorists' base of support. We did not reaffirm our basic values, or secure our homeland.

Instead, we got a color-coded politics of fear. Patriotism as the possession of one political party. The diplomacy of refusing to talk to other countries. A rigid 20th century ideology that insisted that the 21st century's stateless terrorism could be defeated through the invasion and occupation of a state. A deliberate strategy to misrepresent 9/11 to sell a war against a country that had nothing to do with 9/11.

And so, a little more than a year after that bright September day, I was in the streets of Chicago again, this time speaking at a rally in opposition to war in Iraq. I did not oppose all wars, I said. I was a strong supporter of the war in Afghanistan. But I said I could not support 'a dumb war, a rash war' in Iraq. I worried about a 'US occupation of undetermined length, at undetermined cost, with undetermined consequences' in the heart of the Muslim world. I pleaded that we 'finish the fight with bin Ladin and Al Qaeda'.

The political winds were blowing in a different direction. The President was determined to go to war. There was just one obstacle: the US Congress. Nine days after I spoke, that obstacle was removed. Congress rubber-stamped the rush to war, giving the President the broad and open-ended authority he uses to this day. With that vote, Congress became co-author of a catastrophic war. And we went off to fight on the wrong battlefield, with no appreciation of how many enemies we would create, and no plan for how to get out.

Because of a war in Iraq that should never have been authorized and should never have been waged, we are now less safe than we were before 9/11.

According to the National Intelligence Estimate, the threat to our homeland from Al Qaeda is 'persistent and evolving'. Iraq is a training ground for terror, torn apart by civil war. Afghanistan is more violent than it has been since 2001. Al

Qaeda has a sanctuary in Pakistan. Israel is besieged by emboldened enemies, talking openly of its destruction. Iran is now presenting the broadest strategic challenge to the United States in the Middle East in a generation. Groups affiliated with or inspired by Al Qaeda operate worldwide. Six years after 9/11, we are again in the midst of a 'summer of threat', with bin Ladin and many more terrorists determined to strike in the United States.

What's more, in the dark halls of Abu Ghraib and the detention cells of Guantanamo, we have compromised our most precious values. What could have been a call to a generation has become an excuse for unchecked presidential power. A tragedy that united us was turned into a political wedge issue used to divide us.

It is time to turn the page. It is time to write a new chapter in our response to 9/11.

Just because the President misrepresents our enemies does not mean we do not have them. The terrorists are at war with us. The threat is from violent extremists who are a small minority of the world's 1.3 billion Muslims, but the threat is real. They distort Islam. They kill man, woman and child; Christian and Hindu, Jew and Muslim. They seek to create a repressive caliphate. To defeat this enemy, we must understand who we are fighting against, and what we are fighting for.

The President would have us believe that every bomb in Baghdad is part of Al Qaeda's war against us, not an Iraqi civil war. He elevates Al Qaeda in Iraq – which didn't exist before our invasion – and overlooks the people who hit us on 9/11, who are training new recruits in Pakistan. He lumps together groups with very different goals: Al Qaeda and Iran, Shiite militias and Sunni insurgents. He confuses our mission.

And worse – he is fighting the war the terrorists want us to fight. Bin Ladin and his allies know they cannot defeat us on the field of battle or in a genuine battle of ideas. But they can provoke the reaction we've seen in Iraq: a misguided invasion of a Muslim country that sparks new insurgencies, ties down our military, busts our budgets, increases the pool of terrorist recruits, alienates America, gives democracy a bad name, and prompts the American people to question our engagement in the world.

By refusing to end the war in Iraq, President Bush is giving the terrorists what they really want, and what the Congress voted to give them in 2002: a US occupation of undetermined length, at undetermined cost, with undetermined consequences.

It is time to turn the page. When I am President, we will wage the war that has to be won, with a comprehensive strategy with five elements: getting out of Iraq and on to the right battlefield in Afghanistan and Pakistan; developing the capabilities and partnerships we need to take out the terrorists and the world's most deadly weapons; engaging the world to dry up support for terror and extremism; restoring our values; and securing a more resilient homeland.

The first step must be getting off the wrong battlefield in Iraq, and taking the fight to the terrorists in Afghanistan and Pakistan.

I introduced a plan in January that would have already started bringing our troops out of Iraq, with a goal of removing all combat brigades by March 31, 2008. If the President continues to veto this plan, then ending this war will be my first priority when I take office.

There is no military solution in Iraq. Only Iraq's leaders can settle the grievances at the heart of Iraq's civil war. We must apply pressure on them to act, and our best leverage is reducing our troop presence. And we must also do the hard and sustained diplomatic work in the region on behalf of peace and stability.

In ending the war, we must act with more wisdom than we started it. That is why my plan would maintain sufficient forces in the region to target Al Qaeda within Iraq. But we must recognize that Al Qaeda is not the primary source of violence in Iraq, and has little support – not from Shia and Kurds who Al Qaeda has targeted, or Sunni tribes hostile to foreigners. On the contrary, Al Qaeda's appeal within Iraq is enhanced by our troop presence.

Ending the war will help isolate Al Qaeda and give Iraqis the incentive and opportunity to take them out. It will also allow us to direct badly needed resources to Afghanistan. Our troops have fought valiantly there, but Iraq has deprived them of the support they need – and deserve. As a result, parts of Afghanistan are falling into the hands of the Taliban, and a mix of terrorism, drugs, and corruption threatens to overwhelm the country.

As President, I would deploy at least two additional brigades to Afghanistan to re-enforce our counter-terrorism operations and support Nato's efforts against the Taliban. As we step up our commitment, our European friends must do the same, and without the burdensome restrictions that have hampered Nato's efforts. We must also put more of an Afghan face on security by improving the training and equipping of the Afghan Army and Police, and including Afghan soldiers in US and Nato operations.

We must not, however, repeat the mistakes of Iraq. The solution in Afghanistan is not just military – it is political and economic. As President, I would increase our non-military aid by $1 billion. These resources should fund projects at the local level to impact ordinary Afghans, including the development of alternative livelihoods for poppy farmers. And we must seek better performance from the Afghan government, and support that performance through tough anti-corruption safeguards on aid, and increased international support to develop the rule of law across the country.

Above all, I will send a clear message: we will not repeat the mistake of the past, when we turned our back on Afghanistan following Soviet withdrawal. As 9/11 showed us, the security of Afghanistan and America is shared. And today, that security is most threatened by the Al Qaeda and Taliban sanctuary in the tribal regions of north-west Pakistan.

Al Qaeda terrorists train, travel, and maintain global communications in this safe-haven. The Taliban pursues a hit and run strategy, striking in Afghanistan, then skulking across the border to safety.

This is the wild frontier of our globalized world. There are wind-swept deserts and cave-dotted mountains. There are tribes that see borders as nothing more than lines on a map, and governments as forces that come and go. There are blood ties deeper than alliances of convenience, and pockets of extremism that follow religion to violence. It's a tough place.

But that is no excuse. There must be no safe-haven for terrorists who threaten America. We cannot fail to act because action is hard.

As President, I would make the hundreds of millions of dollars in US military aid to Pakistan conditional, and I would make our conditions clear: Pakistan must make substantial progress in closing down the training camps, evicting foreign fighters, and preventing the Taliban from using Pakistan as a staging area for attacks in Afghanistan.

I understand that President Musharraf has his own challenges. But let me make this clear. There are terrorists holed up in those mountains who murdered 3,000 Americans. They are plotting to strike again. It was a terrible mistake to fail to act when we had a chance to take out an Al Qaeda leadership meeting in 2005. If we have actionable intelligence about high-value terrorist targets and President Musharraf won't act, we will.

And Pakistan needs more than F-16s to combat extremism. As the Pakistani government increases investment in secular education to counter radical madrasas, my Administration will increase America's commitment. We must help Pakistan invest in the provinces along the Afghan border, so that the extremists' program of hate is met with one of hope. And we must not turn a blind eye to elections that are neither free nor fair – our goal is not simply an ally in Pakistan, it is a democratic ally.

Beyond Pakistan, there is a core of terrorists – probably in the tens of thousands – who have made their choice to attack America. So the second step in my strategy will be to build our capacity and our partnerships to track down, capture or kill terrorists around the world, and to deny them the world's most dangerous weapons.

I will not hesitate to use military force to take out terrorists who pose a direct threat to America. This requires a broader set of capabilities, as outlined in the Army and Marine Corps's new counter-insurgency manual. I will ensure that our military becomes more stealthy, agile, and lethal in its ability to capture or kill terrorists. We need to recruit, train, and equip our armed forces to better target terrorists, and to help foreign militaries to do the same. This must include a program to bolster our ability to speak different languages, understand different cultures, and coordinate complex missions with our civilian agencies.

To succeed, we must improve our civilian capacity. The finest military in the world is adapting to the challenges of the 21st century. But it cannot counter insurgent and terrorist threats without civilian counterparts who can carry out economic and political reconstruction missions – sometimes in dangerous places. As President, I will strengthen these civilian capacities, recruiting our best and brightest to take on this challenge. I will increase both the numbers and capabilities of our diplomats, development experts, and other civilians who can work alongside our military. We can't just say there is no military solution to these problems. We need to integrate all aspects of American might.

One component of this integrated approach will be new Mobile Development Teams that bring together personnel from the State Department, the Pentagon, and USAID. These teams will work with civil society and local governments to make an immediate impact in peoples' lives, and to turn the tide against extremism. Where people are most vulnerable, where the light of hope has grown dark, and where we are in a position to make a real difference in advancing security and opportunity – that is where these teams will go.

I will also strengthen our intelligence. This is about more than an organizational chart. We need leadership that forces our agencies to share information, and leadership that never – ever – twists the facts to support bad policies. But we must also build our capacity to better collect and analyze information, and to carry out operations to disrupt terrorist plots and break up terrorist networks.

This cannot just be an American mission. Al Qaeda and its allies operate in nearly 100 countries. The United States cannot steal every secret, penetrate every cell, act on every tip, or track down every terrorist – nor should we have to do this alone. This is not just about our security. It is about the common security of all the world.

As President, I will create a Shared Security Partnership Program to forge an international intelligence and law enforcement infrastructure to take down terrorist networks from the remote islands of Indonesia, to the sprawling cities of Africa. This program will provide $5 billion over three years for counter-terrorism cooperation with countries around the world, including information sharing, funding for training, operations, border security, anti-corruption programs, technology, and targeting terrorist financing. And this effort will focus on helping our partners succeed without repressive tactics, because brutality breeds terror, it does not defeat it.

We must also do more to safeguard the world's most dangerous weapons. We know Al Qaeda seeks a nuclear weapon. We know they would not hesitate to use one. Yet there is still about 50 tons of highly enriched uranium, some of it poorly secured, at civilian nuclear facilities in over forty countries. There are still about 15,000 to 16,000 nuclear weapons and stockpiles of uranium and plutonium scattered across 11 time zones in the former Soviet Union.

That is why I worked in the Senate with Dick Lugar to pass a law that would help the United States and our allies detect and stop the smuggling of weapons of mass destruction. That is why I am introducing a bill with Chuck Hagel that seeks to prevent nuclear terrorism, reduce global nuclear arsenals, and stop the spread of nuclear weapons. And that is why, as President, I will lead a global effort to secure all nuclear weapons and material at vulnerable sites within four years. While we work to secure existing stockpiles, we should also negotiate a verifiable global ban on the production of new nuclear weapons material.

And I won't hesitate to use the power of American diplomacy to stop countries from obtaining these weapons or sponsoring terror. The lesson of the Bush years is that not talking does not work. Go down the list of countries we've ignored and see how successful that strategy has been. We haven't talked to Iran, and they continue to build their nuclear program. We haven't talked to Syria, and they continue support for terror. We tried not talking to North Korea, and they now have enough material for six to eight more nuclear weapons.

It's time to turn the page on the diplomacy of tough talk and no action. It's time to turn the page on Washington's conventional wisdom that agreement must be reached before you meet, that talking to other countries is some kind of reward, and that Presidents can only meet with people who will tell them what they want to hear.

President Kennedy said it best: 'Let us never negotiate out of fear, but let us never fear to negotiate'. Only by knowing your adversary can you defeat them or drive wedges between them. As President, I will work with our friends and allies, but I won't outsource our diplomacy in Tehran to the Europeans, or our diplomacy in Pyongyang to the Chinese. I will do the careful preparation needed, and let these countries know where America stands. They will no longer have the excuse of American intransigence. They will have our terms: no support for terror and no nuclear weapons.

But America must be about more than taking out terrorists and locking up weapons, or else new terrorists will rise up to take the place of every one we capture or kill. That is why the third step in my strategy will be drying up the rising well of support for extremism.

When you travel to the world's trouble spots as a United States Senator, much of what you see is from a helicopter. So you look out, with the buzz of the rotor in your ear, maybe a door gunner nearby, and you see the refugee camp in Darfur, the flood near Djibouti, the bombed out block in Baghdad. You see thousands of desperate faces.

Al Qaeda's new recruits come from Africa and Asia, the Middle East and Europe. Many come from disaffected communities and disconnected corners of our interconnected world. And it makes you stop and wonder: when those faces look up at an American helicopter, do they feel hope, or do they feel hate?

We know where extremists thrive. In conflict zones that are incubators of resentment and anarchy. In weak states that cannot control their borders or territory, or meet the basic needs of their people. From Africa to central Asia to the Pacific Rim – nearly 60 countries stand on the brink of conflict or collapse. The extremists encourage the exploitation of these hopeless places on their hate-filled websites.

And we know what the extremists say about us. America is just an occupying Army in Muslim lands, the shadow of a shrouded figure standing on a box at Abu Ghraib, the power behind the throne of a repressive leader. They say we are at war with Islam. That is the whispered line of the extremist who has nothing to offer in this battle of ideas but blame – blame America, blame progress, blame Jews. And often he offers something along with the hate. A sense of empowerment. Maybe an education at a madrasa, some charity for your family, some basic services in the neighborhood. And then: a mission and a gun.

We know we are not who they say we are. America is at war with terrorists who killed on our soil. We are not at war with Islam. America is a compassionate nation that wants a better future for all people. The vast majority of the world's 1.3 billion Muslims have no use for bin Ladin or his bankrupt ideas. But too often since 9/11, the extremists have defined us, not the other way around.

When I am President, that will change. We will author our own story.

We do need to stand for democracy. And I will. But democracy is about more than a ballot box. America must show – through deeds as well as words – that we stand with those who seek a better life. That child looking up at the helicopter must see America and feel hope.

As President, I will make it a focus of my foreign policy to roll back the tide of hopelessness that gives rise to hate. Freedom must mean freedom from fear, not the freedom of anarchy. I will never shrug my shoulders and say – as Secretary Rumsfeld did – 'Freedom is untidy'. I will focus our support on helping nations build independent judicial systems, honest police forces, and financial systems that are transparent and accountable. Freedom must also mean freedom from want, not freedom lost to an empty stomach. So I will make poverty reduction a key part of helping other nations reduce anarchy.

I will double our annual investments to meet these challenges to $50 billion by 2012. And I will support a $2 billion Global Education Fund to counter the radical madrasas – often funded by money from within Saudi Arabia – that have filled young minds with messages of hate. We must work for a world where every child, everywhere, is taught to build and not to destroy. And as we lead we will ask for more from our friends in Europe and Asia as well – more support for our diplomacy, more support for multilateral peacekeeping, and more support to rebuild societies ravaged by conflict.

I will also launch a program of public diplomacy that is a coordinated effort across my Administration, not a small group of political officials at the State Department explaining a misguided war. We will open 'America Houses' in cities across the Islamic world, with Internet, libraries, English lessons, stories of America's Muslims and the strength they add to our country, and vocational programs. Through a new 'America's Voice Corps' we will recruit, train, and send out into the field talented young Americans who can speak with – and listen to – the people who today hear about us only from our enemies.

As President, I will lead this effort. In the first 100 days of my Administration, I will travel to a major Islamic forum and deliver an address to redefine our struggle. I will make clear that we are not at war with Islam, that we will stand with those who are willing to stand up for their future, and that we need their effort to defeat the prophets of hate and violence. I will speak directly to that child who looks up at that helicopter, and my message will be clear: 'You matter to us. Your future is our future. And our moment is now.'

This brings me to the fourth step in my strategy: I will make clear that the days of compromising our values are over.

Major General Paul Eaton had a long and distinguished career serving this country. It included training the Iraqi Army. After Abu Ghraib, his senior Iraqi advisor came into his office and said: 'You have no idea how this will play out on the streets of Baghdad and the rest of the Arab world. How can this be?' This was not the America he had looked up to.

As the counter-insurgency manual reminds us, we cannot win a war unless we maintain the high ground and keep the people on our side. But because the Administration decided to take the low road, our troops have more enemies. Because the Administration cast aside international norms that reflect American values, we are less able to promote our values. When I am President, America will reject torture without exception. America is the country that stood against that kind of behaviour, and we will do so again.

I also will reject a legal framework that does not work. There has been only one conviction at Guantanamo. It was for a guilty plea on material support for terrorism. The sentence was 9 months. There has not been one conviction of a terrorist act. I have faith in America's courts, and I have faith in our Judges Advocate General (JAGs). As President, I will close Guantanamo, reject the Military Commissions Act, and adhere to the Geneva Conventions. Our Constitution and our Uniform Code of Military Justice provide a framework for dealing with the terrorists.

This Administration also puts forward a false choice between the liberties we cherish and the security we demand. I will provide our intelligence and law enforcement agencies with the tools they need to track and take out the terrorists without undermining our Constitution and our freedom.

That means no more illegal wire-tapping of American citizens. No more national security letters to spy on citizens who are not suspected of a crime. No more tracking citizens who do nothing more than protest a misguided war. No more ignoring the law when it is inconvenient. That is not who we are. And it is not what is necessary to defeat the terrorists. The Foreign Intelligence Surveillance Act court works. The separation of powers works. Our Constitution works. We will again set an example for the world that the law is not subject to the whims of stubborn rulers, and that justice is not arbitrary.

This Administration acts like violating civil liberties is the way to enhance our security. It is not. There are no short-cuts to protecting America, and that is why the fifth part of my strategy is doing the hard and patient work to secure a more resilient homeland.

Too often this Administration's approach to homeland security has been to scatter money around and avoid hard choices, or to scare Americans without telling them what to be scared of, or what to do. A Department set up to make Americans feel safer didn't even show up when bodies drifted through the streets in New Orleans. That's not acceptable.

My Administration will take an approach to homeland security guided by risk. I will establish a Quadrennial Review at the Department of Homeland Security – just like at the Pentagon – to undertake a top to bottom review of the threats we face and our ability to confront them. And I will develop a comprehensive National Infrastructure Protection Plan that draws on both local know-how and national priorities.

We have to put resources where our infrastructure is most vulnerable. That means tough and permanent standards for securing our chemical plants. Improving our capability to screen cargo and investing in safeguards that will prevent the disruption of our ports. And making sure our energy sector – our refineries and pipelines and power grids – is protected so that terrorists cannot cripple our economy.

We also have to get past a top-down approach. Folks across America are the ones on the front lines. On 9/11, it was citizens – empowered by their knowledge of the World Trade Center attacks – who protected our government by heroically taking action on Flight 93 to keep it from reaching our nation's capital. When I have information that can empower Americans, I will share it with them.

Information sharing with state and local governments must be a two-way street, because we never know where the two pieces of the puzzle are that might fit together – the tip from Afghanistan, and the cop who sees something suspicious on Michigan Avenue. I will increase funding to help train police to gather information and connect it to the intelligence they receive from the federal government. I will address the problem in our prisons, where the most disaffected and disconnected Americans are being explicitly targeted for conversion by Al Qaeda and its ideological allies.

And my Administration will not permit more lives to be lost because emergency responders are not outfitted with the communications capability and protective equipment their job requires, or because the federal government is too slow to respond when disaster strikes. We've been through that on 9/11. We've been through it during Katrina. I will ensure that we have the resources and competent federal leadership we need to support our communities when American lives are at stake.

But this effort can't just be about what we ask of our men and women in uniform. It can't just be about how we spend our time or our money.

It's about the kind of country we are.

We are in the early stages of a long struggle. Yet since 9/11, we've heard a lot about what America can't do or shouldn't do or won't even try. We can't vote against a misguided war in Iraq because that would make us look weak, or talk to other countries because that would be a reward. We can't reach out to the hundreds of millions of Muslims who reject terror because we worry they hate us. We can't protect the homeland because there are too many targets, or secure our people while staying true to our values. We can't get past the America of Red and Blue, the politics of who's up and who's down.

That is not the America that I know.

The America I know is the last, best hope for that child looking up at a helicopter. It's the country that put a man on the moon; that defeated fascism and helped rebuild Europe. It's a country whose strength abroad is measured not just by armies, but rather by the power of our ideals, and by our purpose to forge an ever more perfect union at home.

That's the America I know. We just have to act like it again to write that next chapter in the American story. If we do, we can keep America safe while extending security and opportunity around the world. We can hold true to our values, and in doing so advance those values abroad. And we can be what that child looking up at a helicopter needs us to be: the relentless opponent of terror and tyranny, and the light of hope to the world.

To make this story reality, it's going to take Americans coming together and changing the fundamental direction of this country. It's going to take the service of a new generation of young people. It's going to take facing tragedy head-on and turning it into the next generation's triumph. That is a challenge that I welcome. Because when we do make that change, we'll do more than win a war – we'll live up to that calling to make America, and the world, safer, freer, and more hopeful than we found it.

As prepared for delivery

COMMUNICATION WORKERS UNION

May Day Greetings

No Trident replacement

Billy Hayes
General Secretary

Jane Loftus
President

Turbulence in the Global Balkans

Zbigniew Brzezinski

On 1 February 2008, Zbigniew Brzezinski was interviewed by James Naughtie on Radio 4's Today programme. A longer version of the interview was posted on the programme's website. This is what the former National Security Advisor to President Carter said.

BBC: Let me ask you a very straightforward question. What is the biggest problem in international affairs, from an American perspective, facing the next president of the United States?

ZB: I think the overall response pertains to global turbulence because we are now in a phase in which all of mankind is politically activated and restless. But the specific focus of that restlessness is in an area that ranges from the Sinai Peninsula, between Egypt and Israel, to Shenyang, China's western most province; from South Russia to the Indian Ocean. I call that area the Global Balkans – the modern equivalent of the European Balkans – and that is the area of the greatest turmoil and the area which poses the greatest threat to global stability.

BBC: And the comparison with the Balkans, in the role that that area has played in European history, is rather a melancholy one, isn't it?

ZB: Yes, because the Balkans have had a suction effect on external powers, drawing them into the conflict. I don't expect a conflict between the major powers arising in the Global Balkans but I think there is a real risk that the United States could be drawn into a conflict which expands in scale, in geographical reach and then undermines America's ability to play a constructive world role, with very damaging consequences for the West in general, specifically for the EU, and very destabilising consequences for all of the other major players in the world.

BBC: So what are the mistakes, in your view, that need to be avoided and what needs to be done?

ZB: In a nutshell I think we need to be more active, more constructive, more engaged in seeking an Israeli/Palestinian accommodation because that conflict radicalises the Middle

East. We have to be willing to recognise the fact that enduring American occupation of Iraq is no solution because we are no longer in a colonial or imperial age. We have to be prepared to negotiate seriously with Iran. And we have to avoid over-militarising our engagement in Afghanistan, and potentially Pakistan, because that could then backfire against us.

BBC: Let me begin to go through that. You talk about the Israel/Palestine problem having radicalised, or having the capacity to radicalise, the Middle East. The problem is that has already happened.

ZB: You can't use the past tense on it because that implies a kind of terminal conclusion. It is happening. The Middle East is being radicalised and destabilised, but it's a process and it's a process that should be reversed.

BBC: Can it be reversed?

ZB: I think so. I think if there was a breakthrough in the Israeli/Palestinian conflict, if there was a settlement that was equitable, that paves the way for eventual reconciliation that in turn permits Israel to become the Singapore of the Middle East, working together with the Palestinians and the Arabs, I think it can be reversed.

BBC: But you know, better than anyone, that the essential deal, the outlines of a deal have been on the table for, let us say, 10 or 15 years. So, everyone knows what they are, we can argue about the edges, about the status of Jerusalem, or about the West Bank, or the Right of Return, but the essence of the package is there. What could a new President do to make that work in a way that, for example, President Clinton and then President Bush have failed to do?

ZB: What you could do is become directly engaged in facilitating a reconciliation, a settlement, in which the first needed step is a compromise formula for both sides. As long as the United States stays on the sidelines neither of the two parties is inclined to step forward and begin the negotiating process by making a significant concession because it fears, quite naturally, that the other side will quite simply pocket it. So we have a stalemate. President Bush has said repeatedly that he expects a settlement this year. If he is serious about it, he will have to be engaged directly. If he is not, it will be up to his successor to do so.

BBC: What is your reading of the consequences of the foreign policy pursued by the two Bush terms as we come to their end?

ZB: I have written a book which has dealt with this, the book is entitled *Second Chance*, and there is a chapter in it entitled 'Catastrophic Leadership'. I think President Bush's leadership internationally has been catastrophic for the United

States, in the sense that it de-legitimated America's world role, it undermined the credibility of the American President. It has stirred up an enormous amount of animosity toward the United States and that has to be undone.

BBC: Do you think it should be undone, because it's a different kind of world now? China is emerging; India is emerging in a different way. Do you think that America could, or should, regain the kind of role that it once thought it had?

ZB: I think it could regain a constructive pre-eminent role but I think we all have to be aware of the fact that preponderance is not omnipotence, that preponderance does not justify a recall to arms, preponderance does not create the grounds for a policy based on the proposition 'if you're not with us, you're against us'.

BBC: But isn't the problem this: that many American people have come to believe that that is not true and the opposite is true? And they need to be argued with in the way that you suggest?

ZB: That's right. That's what the presidential elections are going to be all about. I think we are going to have a very clear choice this time between a Democrat, we don't yet know who it will be but a Democrat will more or less say what I have been saying, although one of the two competing Democrats is more inclined to talk in those terms, and a Republican who in all probability will be talking a great deal about the war on terror, about Jihad, or as the President said the other day in the State of the Union message, that the defining ideological challenge of the 21st century is the war on terror. Now I ask you, could anyone in the year 1908 predict what the defining ideological challenge would be in the 20th century? Or in 1808 of the 19th century? That's what this debate will be about.

BBC: This gets us to the meat of it. Because Senator McCain, who's now head of the pack and may well be the nominee, we don't know that, but he may well be the nominee for the Republican Party, says that the greatest challenge to the United States of the 21st century, the first challenge, he does go as far as you've just gone ...

ZB: It's not me; it was President Bush who said it.

BBC: ... no, I know, I understand, but he doesn't go as far as that, he says the first challenge of the 21st century is Jihadist Islamic terrorism. Now, how do you advise a presidential candidate on the other side, and you are a supporter of Barack Obama, to counter that argument? What should he say in response?

ZB: Largely by saying what I said at the very opening of the discussion. Namely, that the world is very turbulent, in general there is a great deal of restlessness with global inequalities, and there is a particular region of the world which is rammed by conflicts and we have to be very careful in how we deal with them, so that we don't over-militarise them and become bogged down in them. That is precisely the issue and to elevate the Jihad into the major confrontation of our time reminds me of the people who used to talk about the Crusades. We didn't call the war against Hitler a crusade. We didn't call the Cold War a crusade. We have to have a sense of balance in our analysis and I'm agreeing with you that the debate of the presidential campaign is going to be precisely over that excessive, in my judgement, and misleading terminology.

BBC: Let me ask you two questions, one about Iraq and one about Senator Obama. What makes you believe that Senator Obama, with no experience in foreign affairs, with relatively a short time in Washington, with a mind which is sharp, as everyone knows, but with little experience, could lead the United States in these turbulent times as you describe.

ZB: You know this business about lack of experience in foreign affairs is a red herring. What experience did Lincoln have? In recent times, what experience did President Truman have when he became President after a few months as Vice President and having served previously as a Senator from Missouri, from a political machine incidentally? What experience did Clinton have? What is essential to a President is an understanding of the historical moment; of understanding what are the decisive forces at work in the world and understanding how America has to relate itself to these circumstances.

BBC: And you think he has got that?

ZB: I have talked to him a lot. I have a deep conviction that he has that and this is why I think he is the man of the moment.

BBC: In this campaign he is going to have to deal very directly with very specific questions about Iraq, especially if Senator McCain, who's got deep knowledge of these matters, is the candidate on the Republican side. Now precisely what do you think Senator Obama should say about Iraq and, if he were the nominee, what would he say?

ZB: I'm not going to go into that in great detail because our time is running out right now, but let me say that in general what he says on the subject is responsive to the prevailing, dominant view in America that the war in the first place was a fundamental mistake, justified by premises which were false and that it is in the American interest to bring it intelligently to an end. Which means a series of steps to disengage militarily, complemented by a series of political initiatives designed to create a political balance within Iraq and a more constructive interest, on the part of Iraq's neighbours, in Iraq remaining stable, and that can only be galvanised by a political process that is pointed towards the end of an occupation which has all the earmarks of a colonial presence in the post-colonial age.

War on Terror

A Mission Impossible

Paul Rogers

Paul Rogers is Professor of Peace Studies at the University of Bradford. His most recent book is Why We're Losing the War on Terror *(Polity £12.99).*

The military and political problems of United States and coalition policy in Afghanistan and Iraq are causing fresh uncertainty and dispute in Western capitals. This short-term concern, however, must be seen against the background of the entire war on terror – and the American unilateralism that propelled it – since its launch in the aftermath of the events of 11 September 2001.

In the months before 9/11, the neo-conservative euphoria in Washington was already at its height. George W Bush had been in the White House since January 2001 and the administration was developing a clear unilateralist agenda in pursuit of the 'new American century'. This was apparent in its attitude to international agreements: there was no chance of the United States ratifying the comprehensive test ban treaty (CTBT); opposition to the strengthening of the biological and toxin weapons convention (BTWC) and plans for an agreement to prevent the weaponisation of space; determination to avoid joining the International Criminal Court (ICC); and near-certainty that the US would withdraw from the 1972 anti-ballistic missile (ABM) treaty. In this context, the US's sudden withdrawal from the Kyoto climate-change protocol – though it was most surprising to many European governments – was quite consistent with this overall approach.

The power and influence of the neo-conservatives in the new administration mean that all these developments should have been expected. One of the most readable of the neocon commentators, Charles Krauthammer, put it very plainly in an article published just three months before 9/11:

'Multipolarity, yes, when there is no alternative. But not when there is. Not when we have the unique imbalance of power that we enjoy today – and that has given the international system a stability and essential tranquility that it had not known for at least a century.

The international environment is far more

likely to enjoy peace under a single hegemon. Moreover, we are not just any hegemon. We run a uniquely benign imperium.' (see 'The Bush Doctrine: ABM, Kyoto and the New American Unilateralism', *Weekly Standard*, 4 June 2001).

In light of this outlook and its influence at the time, it is hardly a surprise that the shock of the 9/11 attacks resulted in a massive military response, immediately in Afghanistan and later in Iraq. Some commentators advocated another approach – intense international cooperation to bring the Al Qaeda leadership to justice, however long it might take, at the same time as warning against an immediate recourse to regime termination (see, for example, my openDemocracy article 'Afghanistan: the problem with military action', 26 September 2001).

There were other voices, especially from the majority world, that sought a more fundamental change in policy. Walden Bello's is a notable example – writing in late September 2001, he condemned the attacks unreservedly but warned against a heavy military response. Instead, he called for a radical change in outlook:

> 'The only response that will really contribute to global security and peace is for Washington to address not the symptoms of terrorism. It is for the United States to re-examine and substantially change its policies in the Middle East and the Third World, supporting a change in arrangements that will not stand in the way of the achievement of equity, justice and genuine national sovereignty for currently marginalized peoples. Any other way leads to endless war' (see 'Endless War?', *Focus on the Global South*, September 2001).

Such a change would not come from the Bush administration; as a result, the world is now into the seventh year of the 'long war'. From this distance and in view of all that has happened in these years, Bello's prognosis looks uncomfortably accurate. Moreover, the United States and its small band of coalition states is mired in Iraq, and a larger if unhappy coalition anticipates years of conflict in Afghanistan.

The true path

It is still just possible that there will be some US troop withdrawals from Iraq in 2008, though the chances are becoming remote. In any case, any drawdown will do no more than take the numbers to the levels of 2003-06 – before the start of the 2007 surge. Meanwhile the United States is consolidating its influence over Iraq's political and economic life while developing several massive military bases and pulling in more air power to maintain control (see my openDemocracy article 'The Iraq project', 31 January 2008). Unless there is a quite extraordinary change in policy, the United States will be in Iraq for very many years to come; the importance of the region's oil resources alone helps ensure that.

In Afghanistan, there is considerable disunity among Nato member-states. The flurry of diplomatic activity – including US defence secretary Robert M Gates's criticism of Nato allies, and the visit of US secretary of state Condoleezza Rice and Britain's foreign secretary David Miliband to Kabul on 7 February – reflects the extent and immediacy of concern about the problems they are facing (see Ann Scott

Tyson & Josh White, 'Gates Hits Nato Allies' Role in Afghanistan', *Washington Post*, 7 February 2008). Gordon Brown's government is seen as the key ally at present and there is concern in Washington that London may find public opinion turning against British involvement in Afghanistan. Britain has by far the largest involvement of any of Nato's European member-states; on 6 February, its defence minister Des Browne announced that most of the élite Parachute regiment would be deployed to Helmand province for the period of April-October 2008.

For the United States this continuing involvement is crucial, but it is still not enough – given the reluctance of many Nato states to put their own troops on the frontline. The Pentagon declared its intention on 15 January 2008 to add 3,200 marines to its own forces in the country, but there are calls for much larger increases. One of Washington's leading conservative think-tanks, the American Enterprise Institute, was a key instigator of the 2007 surge in Iraq; it now wants a similar surge in Afghanistan involving the immediate transfer there of another three combat brigades. Along with support troops and the extra marines already assigned, this would take the number of foreign troops in Afghanistan to around 70,000; it would also involve substantial reinforcements of air power.

A calculation of the current force levels in Afghanistan and Iraq, with the large contingents of private-security contractors included, suggests that there will soon be close to 250,000 foreign military personnel occupying the two countries; and they are backed up by almost as many private civilian employees.

The term 'occupying' and 'occupation' are not in the vocabulary of the White House or 10 Downing Street: from their perspective what is happening is a major security operation to win the war on terror while bringing two key countries safely into the Western orbit. There may be civilian casualties and many other problems but the entire endeavour is, in this perspective, essentially benign – a right and proper response from the civilised countries of the North Atlantic to the appalling atrocity of 11 September 2001.

Krauthammer's 'benign imperium' may look a little tattered around the edges but it remains the basis for coalition action (see my 'US unilateralism – alive and kicking?', 23 January 2002). The fact that some countries within Nato may no longer be fully committed is both sad and annoying, but they cannot be allowed to deter American leadership from the true and correct path.

The blind eye

The problem is twofold. First, most of the world simply does not see things this way. This does not mean that the majority world supports Osama bin Laden and the Al Qaeda movement. True, many more people do so now than before 9/11, but this is not the real significance of what has happened. What has really changed is that the occupation of countries in the Islamic world by Western military forces is simply not feasible. The claims that they are peacekeepers or stabilisers is regarded as untenable by many who point to the many thousands of civilians who have been and are being killed each year, and the tens of thousands of people detained without trial.

Second, the United States-led approach is just not working. It may not have been right for the European colonial powers of recent centuries to occupy much of the world, but it was politically possible for them to do so. Now – although the truth is taking a long time to be recognised – the world is in a very different age. Two changes in particular are decisive. The first is that the world's media (not least in the Arab and Muslim worlds) has opened up and diversified with astonishing rapidity. In little more than a decade, twenty-four-hour TV news channels have taken to the air, offering fresh perspectives and graphic accounts of the occupations. Moreover, the web, broadband, cell-phones and many other communications systems have further added to the range of information available, often including overt and hard-hitting propaganda.

The second change is that asymmetric warfare – especially the ability of the weak to take up arms against the strong – means that the world's most powerful states can no longer maintain control (see my *Losing Control: Global Security in the 21ˢᵗ Century*, Pluto Press, [second edition], 2002). In the fiscal year 2009, the US military budget will be the largest in real terms since the Second World War – exceeding expenditure at the time of the Korean war (1950-53), the Vietnam war (1965-75), or at the height of the Cold War. It will also be larger than that of every other country put together, even excluding direct war costs in Iraq and Afghanistan.

Yet even with all this, and a belief in the rightness of its cause, the reality is that the United States cannot continue – militarily, financially, or politically – to occupy countries such as Iraq and Afghanistan for years to come. The problems are widely recognised and many liberal think-tanks and politicians on both sides of the Atlantic now advocate partial withdrawals from both countries. The latter may have the best of motives, but perhaps they too have not recognised what has changed.

The occupation of countries in the Middle East and South-West Asia by Western military forces is no longer politically feasible. The starting-point for any new policy will have to be complete withdrawal. Any other approach has been rendered obsolete by the cumulative effects of the last six years. That thought is at present beyond Washington and London's reach, but it is a reality that one day they will simply have to face.

With grateful acknowledgements to openDemocracy (www.opendemocracy.net)

Extraordinary Rendition

Britain's Central Role

Ben Griffin

This statement was prepared and read by Ben Griffin, ex-Special Air Service (SAS) soldier, at a press conference in London on 25 February 2008.

Our government would have us believe that our involvement in the process known as Extraordinary Rendition is limited to two occasions on which planes carrying detainees landed to refuel on the British Indian Ocean Territory, Diego Garcia. David Miliband has stated that the British Government expects the Government of the United States to 'seek permission to render detainees via UK territory and airspace, including Overseas Territories; that we will grant that permission only if we are satisfied that the rendition would accord with UK law and our international obligations; and how we understand our obligations under the UN Convention Against Torture'. (Taken from a statement given to the House of Commons by the Foreign Secretary David Miliband on Thursday 21 February 2008.)

The use of British Territory and airspace pales into insignificance in light of the fact that it has been British soldiers detaining the victims of Extraordinary Rendition in the first place. Since the invasion of Afghanistan in the autumn of 2001, United Kingdom Special Forces (UKSF) has operated within a joint US/UK Task Force. This Task Force has been responsible for the detention of hundreds if not thousands of individuals in Afghanistan and Iraq. Individuals detained by British soldiers within this Task Force have ended up in Guantanamo Bay Detention Camp, Bagram Theatre Internment Facility, Balad Special Forces Base, Camp Nama BIAP and Abu Ghraib Prison.

Whilst the government has stated its desire that the Guantanamo Bay detention camp be closed, it has remained silent over these other secretive prisons in Iraq and Afghanistan. These secretive prisons are part of a global network in which individuals face torture and are held indefinitely without charge. All of this is in direct contravention of the Geneva Conventions, International Law and the UN Convention Against Torture.

Early involvement of UK Special Forces in

the process of Extraordinary Rendition centres around operations carried out in Afghanistan in late 2001. Of note is an incident at the Qalai Janghi fortress, near Mazar-i-Sharif. UK Special Forces fought alongside their US counterparts to put down a bloody revolt by captured Taliban fighters. The surviving Taliban fighters were then rendered to Guantanamo Bay.

After the invasion of Iraq in 2003 this joint US/UK task force appeared. Its primary mission was to kill or capture high value targets. Individuals detained by this Task Force often included non-combatants caught up in the search for high value targets. The use of secret detention centres within Iraq has negated the need to use Guantanamo Bay whilst allowing similar practice to go unnoticed.

I have here an account taken from an interpreter interviewed by the organisation Human Rights Watch (http://hrw.org/reports/2006/us0706/2.htm). He was based at the detention and interrogation facility within Camp Nama at Baghdad International Airport during 2004. This facility was used to interrogate individuals captured by the joint US/UK Task Force. In it are the details of numerous breaches of the Geneva Convention and accounts of torture. These breaches were not the actions of rogue elements: the abuse was systematic and sanctioned through the chain of command. This account is corroborated by an investigation carried out by *New York Times* reporters into Camp Nama and the US/UK Task Force, which appeared in the *New York Times* on 19 March 2006. Throughout my time in Iraq I was in no doubt that individuals detained by UK Special Forces and handed over to our American colleagues would be tortured. During my time as member of the US/UK Task Force, three soldiers recounted to me an incident in which they had witnessed the brutal interrogation of two detainees. Partial drowning and an electric cattle prod were used during this interrogation and this amounted to torture. It was the widely held assumption that this would be the fate of any individuals handed over to our America colleagues. My commanding officer at the time expressed his concern to the whole squadron that we were becoming 'the secret police of Baghdad'.

As UK soldiers within this Task Force a policy that we would detain individuals but not arrest them was continually enforced. Since it was commonly assumed by my colleagues that anyone we detained would subsequently be tortured, this policy of detention and not arrest was regarded as a clumsy legal tool used to distance British soldiers from the whole process.

During the many operations conducted to apprehend high value targets, numerous non-combatants were detained and interrogated in direct contravention of the Geneva Convention regarding the treatment of civilians in occupied territories. I have no doubt in my mind that non-combatants I personally detained were handed over to the Americans and subsequently tortured.

The joint US/UK Task Force has broken International Law, contravened the Geneva Conventions and disregarded the UN Convention Against Torture. British soldiers are intimately involved in the actions of this Task Force. Jack Straw, Margaret Beckett David Miliband, Geoff Hoon, Des Browne, Tony Blair, Gordon Brown – in their respective positions over the last five years they must know that

British soldiers have been operating within this joint US/UK task force. They must have been briefed on the actions of this unit.

As the occupiers of Iraq we have a duty to uphold the law, to abide by the Geneva Conventions and the UN Convention Against Torture. We are also responsible for securing the borders of Iraq. On all counts we have failed. The British Army once had a reputation for playing by the rules. That reputation has been tarnished over the last seven years. We have accepted illegality as the norm. I have no doubt that over the coming months and years increasing amounts of information concerning the actions of British soldiers in Iraq and Afghanistan will become public.

Whilst the majority of British Forces have been withdrawn from Iraq, UK Special Forces remain within the US/UK Task Force.

*Torture, according to the United Nations Convention Against Torture, is 'any act by which severe pain or suffering, whether physical or mental, is intentionally inflicted on a person for such purposes as obtaining from him or a third person information or a confession'.

* * *

On the evening of Thursday 28 February, the Ministry of Defence obtained an injunction from the High Court silencing Mr Griffin after he had given a number of interviews to the national press about rendition and torture in Iraq and elsewhere. On 29 February, Mr Justice Openshaw continued the injunction. Ben Griffin commented:

'As of 1940hrs 29/02/08 I have been placed under an injunction preventing me from speaking publicly and publishing material gained as a result of my service in UKSF (SAS).

I will be continuing to collect evidence and opinion on British involvement in extraordinary rendition, torture, secret detentions, extra judicial detention, use of evidence gained through torture, breaches of the Geneva Conventions, breaches of International Law and failure to abide by our obligations as per UN Convention Against Torture. I am carrying on regardless.'

Suspects Held on Diego Garcia

Tony Simpson
Mark Seddon

Tony Simpson works at the Russell Foundation.
Mark Seddon is a journalist with Aljazeera.net, where he filed this story. He was formerly editor of Tribune.

I

Since 2002, the British Government has repeatedly denied that the United States detained people on Diego Garcia, and also refused access to the International Committee of the Red Cross on the basis that there were no prisoners for the ICRC to visit.

First, Baroness Amos, then Bill Rammell MP who succeeded her at the Foreign Office, informed us that 'there was no truth to any of these allegations' that the US was holding suspected terrorists on Diego Garcia. Bill Rammell, in a letter to Ken Coates dated 9 December 2003, added for emphasis that 'we have our own personnel on Diego Garcia who could not fail to be aware if there were any substance to the allegations which you raise, and they, too, assure me that they are without foundation'. But it seems the detainees may have been removed from the island by that time.

The allegations about interrogation and torture of captives held on Diego Garcia first surfaced in the *Washington Post* on 26 December 2002 (see *Spokesman* nos. *77* and *78).* We subsequently sent a copy of Baroness Amos's denial of these allegations to Barton Gellman, one of the journalists responsible for the story. Mr Gellman replied to say:

'Our experience with spokesmen most likely mirrors yours: they persuade themselves sometimes that they avoid a lie (while appearing to call something true false) by using private definitions of ordinary language. The formulation of Baroness Amos might be consistent with a view that those being held are not suspected "terrorists" but perhaps "associates" of some organisation, or that being held aboard ship is not "on" Diego Garcia. (I don't know if they're aboard ship or not.) ... What we have from our sources is that some Al Qaeda suspects are indeed being held and questioned at Diego Garcia. The British Government could go some way to clearing this up by permitting you or us to pay an unrestricted visit ...'

Now, five years later, the substance of the allegations made in the *Washington Post* has at last been corroborated by the UN Special Rapporteur on Torture, Manfred Nowak (see below), who says he received 'credible allegations' that suspects were held on Diego Garcia for up to a month between 2002 and 2003.

Tony Simpson

* * *

II

The United Nations special rapporteur on torture says he has credible evidence that the US used a British territory for the secret detention and transportation of 'terror' suspects. Manfred Nowak's assertion contradicts statements by the UK and US governments that Diego Garcia island was used merely as a refuelling stop for 'renditions'.

Nowak said on Sunday 9 March 2008 that he had received information about detentions on the British island from multiple sources. He said detainees and other sources had told him 'quite a long time ago' that suspects were sent to the remote outpost and kept there between 2002 and 2003. 'I've had a few allegations and, in my opinion, they were credible,' Nowak told The Associated Press, adding that he could not disclose any of his sources.

Nowak said he did not know how many suspects had been held on the island, but prisoners were purportedly kept at Diego Garcia for 'short periods of time'.

The revelations add further pressure on both the US and UK governments to fully disclose activities on Diego Garcia. British legislators are demanding answers over the allegations.

The British government has admitted that the United States had used Diego Garcia as a refuelling stop for the secret transportation and detention of two terror suspects, but it strenuously denies that the island was used to detain 'high value' prisoners under the US extraordinary rendition programme (see box).

But the CIA was recently forced to issue an 'official apology' for two rendition flights containing terror suspects that landed on the US military base on the island,

---

'Contrary to earlier explicit assurances that Diego Garcia had not been used for rendition flights, recent US investigations have now revealed two occasions, both in 2002, when that had in fact occurred. An error in the earlier US records search meant that those cases did not come to light. In both cases, a US plane with a single detainee on board refuelled at the US facility in Diego Garcia. The detainees did not leave the plane, and the US Government have assured us that no US detainees have ever been held on Diego Garcia. US investigations show no record of any other rendition through Diego Garcia or any other overseas territory, or through the UK itself, since then.'

David Miliband, Foreign Secretary,
Statement to House of Commons, 21 February 2008

saying information previously provided 'turned out to be wrong'.

In February 2008, David Miliband, the British Foreign Secretary, revealed in Parliament that recent talks with Condoleezza Rice, the US Secretary of State, indicated two suspects on flights to Guantanamo Bay and Morocco, in 2002, made a stopover at Diego Garcia. But Miliband said the United States had expressly denied that Diego Garcia was a detention centre. Britain is the first Western European government to directly acknowledge that one of its territories was used in the so-called renditions carried out by the US government.

Human rights groups argue that the practice of sending detainees to third-party countries opens the door for the torture and interrogation of suspects outside international law. The European Parliament and the Council of Europe accuse 14 countries of colluding with the CIA to transport terror suspects to clandestine prisons in third countries.

On 6 March 2008, the High Court of England and Wales granted an injunction to prevent Ben Griffin, a former member of the UK's special forces, from making any further disclosures relating to his allegations regarding the use of British territory and airspace for the secret detention and transportation of 'terror' suspects. Following the injunction, Anne FitzGerald, a senior adviser at Amnesty International, the human rights group, said:

'Rather than seeking to silence people who might have credible evidence of alleged human rights violations, which may include war crimes, the UK authorities should be seeking to investigate those allegations. Amnesty International repeatedly makes calls for the UK to ensure that full and independent investigations are carried out wherever there are credible allegations that agents of the UK, including members of the armed forces, may have been responsible for grave violations of human rights law or for war crimes. Those calls all too often go unheeded: ... Amnesty International repeated its call for such an investigation into the UK's alleged involvement in the US-led programme of renditions and secret detention, following official confirmation, after years of denial, that rendition flights did indeed touch down in the UK territory of Diego Garcia. There can be no accountability without transparency: people – including former soldiers – who have information that may constitute evidence of war crimes or of grave human rights violations must be reassured that they can safely make that information public, without fear of punitive legal action against them. If the government of the UK succeeds in gagging Ben Griffin and burying any significant information he may possess, it risks preventing others from coming forward who may have evidence of serious violations.'

Mark Seddon

Good Day, Comrade Shtrum

John Lanchester

In this review article, the distinguished contributor to the London Review of Books, *John Lanchester, considers Vasily Grossman's* Life and Fate, *as translated by Robert Chandler, and now issued in paperback (Vintage, £9.99).*

In *Postmodernism or, The Cultural Logic of Late Capitalism* – a difficult book, but, it seems increasingly clear, the most important critical work of the last twenty years – Fredric Jameson observes that 'the disappearance of the individual subject, along with its formal consequence, the increasing unavailability of the personal style, engender the well-nigh universal practice today of what may be called pastiche'. This thought-provoking assertion captures a truth about the shift from the modern to the postmodern: there is something pastiche-like about a great many contemporary writers, not least those who write in a personal voice which is in itself a variety of pastiche. Vasily Grossman's masterpiece *Life and Fate* is fascinating for many reasons, and one of them is the way in that it is both a pastiche and a personal statement; a conscious, cold-blooded attempt to sum up everything Grossman knew about the Great Patriotic War, and at the same time to rewrite *War and Peace*. Tolstoy's novel was the only book Grossman read during the war, and he read it twice; *War and Peace* hangs over Grossman's book as a template and a lodestar, and the measure of Grossman's achievement is that a comparison between the two books is not grotesque.

Part of what Tolstoy's example did for Grossman was to give him a place on which to stand, a vantage point. We can see this by considering what some English-language writers did with the war. The two British novelists who went off to the war in mid-career in their mid-thirties, Evelyn Waugh and Anthony Powell, both wrote books about what they had seen at first hand, Waugh's war being more overtly interesting (the Commandos, Crete, parachute training, Yugoslavia) but Powell's more typical (garrison duties, staff work, office politics). In America, the writers who went off to war were younger, apprentice meteors. Gore Vidal wrote a small, cool, personal book in *Williwaw*; Norman Mailer attempted in *The Naked and the Dead* to write the Big Novel about the war and ended up writing a kind of pastiche, a strange hybrid of modernist ambition and postmodernist decentredness – a fake, perhaps, but an interesting one.

As Antony Beevor and Luba Vinogradova's's superb book *A Writer at War* makes clear, Grossman saw more of the war than any of them; more than any other writer. He volunteered to fight but, tubby and shortsighted and unathletic as he was, was sent instead to cover the war for *Krasnaya Zvezda*, the army newspaper. In that capacity he was present at the initial collapse of the Russian army in response to Operation Barbarossa, and the rapidity of the German advance very nearly led on more than one occasion to his capture. He covered the counter-attacks of early 1942 and then went south later that year, providentially, so that he was ideally placed to cover the battle of Stalingrad. He repeatedly crossed the Volga to the west bank, home of the 'Stalingrad Academy of Street Fighting', and interviewed everyone from the famous sniper Chekhov to the commander Chuikov. His reports were vivid but also had a flintiness and a realism about death – much more so than in equivalent Anglo-American war writing – and were very popular with the troops. He was in Stalingrad for five months.

As the Russian army advanced westward Grossman travelled with them. He was present at Kursk, the greatest tank battle in history, and when he came to his birthplace of Berdichev in the Ukraine began to understand the full extent of what the Nazis had done. His writing about the Holocaust has a rare freshness, because he was writing at the same moment he was finding out what had happened. It is as if Grossman, an assimilated Jew, became more conscious of his own ethnicity through confronting evidence of the Holocaust.

> 'There are no Jews in the Ukraine. Nowhere – Poltava, Kharkov, Kremenchug, Borispol, Yagotin – in none of the cities, hundreds of towns, or thousands of villages will you see the black, tear-filled eyes of little girls; you will not hear the pained voice of an old woman; you will not see the dark face of a hungry baby. All is silence. Everything is still. A whole people has been brutally murdered.'

Krasnaya Zvezda would not publish that piece – a glimpse of trouble to come. Grossman began to assemble material for what would be the Jewish Anti-Fascist Committee's *Black Book*, detailing Nazi atrocities*. He arrived at Treblinka, and although the death camp had been demolished by the Nazis on Himmler's direct order, he interviewed witnesses and survivors and published the first account of the camps in any language. His article was a remarkable piece of journalistic assiduity, and was of sufficient weight as a piece of evidence to be quoted at the Nuremberg trials. He travelled through Warsaw and Lodz and followed the final assault on Berlin; he was in the city on the day of its capitulation, and on that very day, wandering around the Reichschancellery, went into Hitler's office and took out a selection of his desk stamps – 'The Führer has confirmed', 'The Führer has agreed' and so on. It's difficult to imagine a more definitive closeness to the action

---

* According to Robert Chandler, the *Black Book* has still not been published in Russia.

than that. Quite a few writers covered the war as journalists and covered it well – Liebling, Malaparte, Gellhorn – but no one got anywhere near Grossman for the amount of time he spent at the front and the historic centrality of the actions he witnessed. I'm not sure there has been a parallel in the writing on any other war.

To say that Grossman had a lot of material to work with, when he sat down to write his war novel, would be to understate. So much material; and so many different perspectives; and so many stories to bring to life. Grossman had already written several novels. It would be interesting to know if he considered adopting a fragmentary, impressionistic method for his war book; some of the journalism has a choppy, imagistic technique which is in some respects more modern in feeling than the novel he came to write. But in the event it was Tolstoy he turned to as a model, as much for the sense of a stable moral perspective as for the fictional techniques: an omniscient third-person observer, a panoramic breadth of focus, a plot which uses a central family group as a way of organising a huge cast of characters. Faced with the greatest horrors of the 20th century, Grossman took up a position in the 19th century as a vantage point.

He did not get it right first time. His first big novel about the war, *For a Just Cause*, is regarded by those who have read it as a Socialist Realist dog, in which the characters, no more than 'names with problems', wander round spouting Stalinist clichés. I can't comment directly because it hasn't been translated, but there is something intriguing in the fact that *Life and Fate* is the sequel to this dud; as if cardboard characters – indeed, the same characters – were suddenly and magically to come to life. Grossman had had more time to digest his experiences, and his gradual disillusionment with the Soviet system led him to see the events of the war, and therefore the people who had taken part in it, more clearly.

When *For a Just Cause* came out it was first praised and then, apparently as part of the anti-semitic turn of the times, denounced. Beevor and Vinogradova make the point that Stalin's anti-semitism was less a matter of racist ideology and more a kind of xenophobia. In any case, it bore down heavily on Grossman. Strangely, it might have been this anti-semitism that made his artistic instincts come to life, and therefore made *Life and Fate* into the book it is. Grossman was never a Party member and several people close to him had spent time in prison for political offences – his cousin, his second wife – but he, to use the language of a different set of circumstances, made the choice to 'work within the system'. He did not, however, manage to delude himself in the way that his friend Ilya Ehrenburg did, and became increasingly disillusioned with the Soviet system. The growing anti-semitism of Stalin's later years was a big part of this. In 1952, Grossman was forced to sign a petition condemning the Jewish doctors involved in the notorious non-existent plot; in the novel he assigns a similar humiliation to the scientist and alter ego Viktor Shtrum. In doing so he antedated the anti-semitic campaigns of Stalin's last years and brought them forward into the period of the war. This transposition hints that it may have been his encounters with anti-semitism that galvanised Grossman into seeing through the pieties of *For a Just Cause*, and turned *Life and Fate* into a great novel.

That greatness is to do with scale. This is one of the hardest qualities to demonstrate, and it is made harder by the unpyrotechnic flatness of Grossman's writing; although it has its virtuosities and set pieces, these are at the level of the character sketch rather than the brilliant sentence or flashy paragraph. Once you get used to this, it comes to seem a virtue; there's no writerly showing-off. What there is is an immense depth of feeling and experience.

In addition to his wartime adventures, Grossman knew the Ukraine; the world of factories, where he had worked; the world of science, from his training as a chemist; the world of the Party ideologues, and the world of those they cajoled, arrested and interrogated. He knew prisoners, snipers, starving old ladies, Slavophile bigots, commissars, collaborators, every flavour of ordinary soldier, tankman, fighter pilot, nurse, power-station worker, Tolstoyan, drunk, and cross teenage daughter. His experiences of Soviet society had an immense range, and he tried to get all of it into *Life and Fate*. The novel gives an extraordinary sense of intimacy with an entire culture.

One test of greatness in fiction is unflinchingness, and *Life and Fate* is utterly unflinching, taking the reader both into the prison camps of the Soviet state and the death camps of the Nazis: the latter journey, accompanying a young boy, David, and the woman who looks after him on the journey, Sofya Levinton, I found that I could not reread. The horror is all the more real because we have actually witnessed the gas chambers being built, and an inspection visit by Eichmann.

'A small surprise had been laid on for Eichmann and Liss during their tour of inspection. In the middle of the gas chamber, the engineers had laid a small table with hors d'oeuvres and wine. Reineke invited Eichmann and Liss to sit down.

Eichmann laughed at this charming idea and said: "With the greatest of pleasure."

He gave his cap to his bodyguard and sat down. His large face suddenly took on a look of kindly concentration, the same look that appears on the faces of millions of men as they sit down to a good meal.

Reineke poured out the wine and they all reached for their glasses, waiting for Eichmann to propose a toast.

The tension in this concrete silence, in these full glasses, was so extreme that Liss felt his heart was about to burst. What he wanted was some ringing toast to clear the atmosphere, a toast to the glory of the German ideal. Instead, the tension grew stronger – Eichmann was chewing a sandwich.

"Well, gentlemen?" said Eichmann. "I call that excellent ham!"

"We're waiting for the master of ceremonies to propose a toast," said Liss.

Eichmann raised his glass.

"To the continued success of our work! Yes, that certainly deserves a toast!"

Eichmann was the only man to eat well and drink very little.'

I remember its being said, after the fall of the Berlin Wall, that a novel should be written about the true believers, about the perspective on events of the people who were, and who remained, completely committed to Communism. *Life and Fate* is, among other things, that novel. One of its central characters is a commissar called Krymov. He is a Party enforcer by trade but also a brave, likeable, fundamentally decent man, still in love with his first wife, Zhenya, a member of the Shaposhnikov family, the clan at the heart of *Life and Fate*. Krymov has had experience of the less rational aspects of the Stalinist state; after being encircled by the Germans in the catastrophic early stages of the war, and fighting his way out, he was subject to interrogation by the NKVD – a consequence of Stalin's clinically paranoid reaction to anyone who had been cut off behind German lines. Krymov's faith in the Party was not shaken. As he spends more and more time in Stalingrad, however, he starts to feel the kind of freedom Grossman himself experienced: 'he no longer felt he was a stepson of the age'. But then Krymov is sent to House 6/1, a bombed-out outpost in which Grekov, the crazily courageous, charismatic 'house manager', and his men are holding off the Germans in intense daily and nightly street-fighting. Grekov is manifestly unimpressed by Krymov's mission – to restore Party discipline and correct attitudes – and Krymov, who finds the atmosphere in the house very disturbing, concludes that he has to remove the house manager from his command. During Krymov's first night in the house, however, Grekov shoots him, not fatally, but so that he has to be withdrawn from the front. While convalescing, Krymov does what he feels has to be his duty, and writes a report on his experiences, including a denunciation of Grekov. But what Krymov doesn't know is that while he was in hospital, the Germans launched a massive assault through a tractor factory, and in the course of it House 6/1 was shelled flat and overrun – so that Grekov and his comrades are now, officially, heroes. Krymov's denunciation could not be more badly timed. He is called to a meeting at the underground command post of the 64th Army.

'A staff officer with a captain's green stripes on his greatcoat called out his name. He had followed him from the command post.

Krymov gave him a puzzled look.

"This way please," the captain said quietly, pointing towards the door of a hut.

Krymov walked past the sentry and through the doorway. They entered a room with a large desk and a portrait of Stalin on the plank wall.

Krymov expected the captain to say something like this: "Excuse me, comrade Battalion Commissar, but would you mind taking this report to comrade Toshcheev on the left bank?" Instead, he said:

"Hand over your weapon and your personal documents."

Krymov's reply was confused and meaningless. "But what right ...? Show me your own documents first ...!"

There could be no doubt about what had happened – absurd and senseless though it might be. Krymov came out with the words that had been muttered before by many thousands of people in similar circumstances:

"It's crazy. I don't understand. It must be a misunderstanding."

These words were no longer those of a free man.'

Krymov, the heartbroken commissar, begins his journey through the penal system of the Soviet state. As he falls, he drags down his ex-wife's current lover, a tank commander called Novikov. The filaments of state surveillance and terror reach everywhere, even in the darkest days of the fight against the Nazis.

Life and Fate does not have a central protagonist, but the character closest to the author's heart is perhaps Viktor Shtrum, a physicist whose working life is evoked so convincingly that it is something of an indictment of other writers who use scientists in their fiction. Shtrum is a theoretical physicist, married to Lyudmila Shaposhnikova; in the course of the novel his mother is murdered by the Nazis, and Lyudmila's son by a previous marriage dies in the battle of Stalingrad. Shtrum has a close circle of scientist friends, with whom he has slightly too frank conversations which he later regrets, and there is a question about whether some of his circle are provocateurs or informers; but when he does get into trouble it is because the state is beginning its turn to anti-semitism. Shtrum has made a theoretical breakthrough, connected with his research into the atom, but he begins to find his work denounced as anti-materialistic and un-Russian. Jewish colleagues lose their jobs. His peers are avoiding him, he is clearly not in favour at his laboratory. Shtrum starts to experience the strange freedom of the outsider, the fact that, once disgraced, he no longer has to be so careful about what he says and does – and then the telephone rings. 'Its ringing now made Viktor as anxious as if it were the middle of the night and a telegram had arrived with news of some tragedy.' He takes the receiver:

'Now it was Lyudmila's turn to look questioningly at him. He groped on the table for a pencil and scrawled a few letters on a scrap of paper. Very slowly, not knowing what she was doing, Lyudmila made the sign of the cross first over herself and then over Viktor. Neither of them said a word.

"This is a bulletin from all the radio services of the Soviet Union."

A voice unbelievably similar to the voice that had addressed the nation, the army, the entire world on July 1941, now addressed a solitary individual holding a telephone receiver.

"Good day, comrade Shtrum."

At that moment everything came together in a jumble of half-formed thoughts and feelings – triumph, a sense of weakness, fear that all this might just be some maniac playing a trick on him, pages of closely written manuscript, that endless questionnaire, the Lubyanka …

Viktor knew that his fate was now being settled. He also had a vague sense of loss, as though he had lost something peculiarly dear to him, something good and touching.

"Good day, Iosif Vissarionovich," he said, astonished to hear himself pronouncing such unimaginable words on the telephone.'

Stalin expresses good wishes for Shtrum's work – and in that moment Shtrum's life is transformed. That one call is all it takes. Stalin, the *deus ex machina*, really does have the powers of a god. It is one of the most extraordinary, electric moments in 20th-century literature, far transcending Tolstoy's use of Napoleon in *War and Peace*, but the moral of the incident is yet to come. As soon as Shtrum gains something, he immediately has more to lose, and his corruption is simply effected. With his new status, he is easily inveigled by his boss at the laboratory to sign an anti-semitic petition. Grossman, who signed a similar petition himself, makes it all too easy to empathise with Shtrum's weakness. It is a devastating depiction of the final trick played by a totalitarian state: to destroy people's sense of themselves by giving them a sniff of success and inclusion.

Fate was kinder to Viktor Shtrum than to his creator. Shtrum at least experienced the acclaim to go with his inner sense of betrayal and shame; from the 1952 publication of *For a Just Cause* onwards, Grossman increasingly felt himself a failure and an outcast. The death of Stalin did not herald a golden age of liberty. Grossman put his sense of disillusionment into *Life and Fate*, and it is part of what makes it a great book. He does not propose a one-for-one moral equivalence between Nazi Germany and Soviet Russia – he was too intelligent to do that – but he has no compunction about pointing out similarities when he sees them. The sense that he had nothing much left to lose energised his writing, and when he submitted the work to *Znamya* in 1960 he was braced for trouble. He did not, however, expect it in the form it took: the KGB arrested not the author, but his book. They confiscated every known copy of the manuscript, as well as the drafts, the out-takes, and the typewriter ribbons with which it had been written. Suslov, the Party ideologue, told Grossman that the book would not be published for two hundred years. 'Why should we add your book to the atomic bombs that our enemies are preparing to launch against us?' Quite a compliment, his certainty that the novel would last that long.

Grossman, warned by his friend Semyon Lipkin, had taken precautions. He gave a copy of the manuscript to Lipkin and another to a friend from his student years. Some time later, a microfilm copy of the manuscript was made by Andrei Sakharov and Yelena Bonner, and the microfilm was smuggled to the West in 1970 by Vladimir Voinovich. (It must have been a bit like Celebrity Dissident Pass-the-Parcel.) In 1980 the book was published for the first time; in 1985, Robert Chandler's fine English translation came out, and in 1988 *Zhizn i Sudba* was published in Russia. Its author did not live to see any of this. After the arrest of his book, Grossman wrote the superb novel *Vsë Techët*, available in English as *Forever Flowing*, though Chandler thinks that translation a mistake: he calls the book *Everything Flows* and says that 'this translation should not have been republished. Firstly, it is both clumsy and full of errors. Secondly, it is based on an incomplete manuscript. Grossman's final, considerably expanded text was published in the Soviet Union in the late 1980s. A translation of that text is long overdue!' Nonetheless, the novel has a real freshness and power: it tells the story of Ivan Grigoryevich, who returns to civilian life in the Soviet Union after thirty years in the gulag. The vision of mid-1950s Russia, seen through his eyes, as a luxurious materialistic paradise, a world of 'parquet floors, glass-enclosed bookcases, paintings and chandeliers', is startling – you can't help but wonder what Ivan Grigoryevich would make of Moscow today. The book is as comprehensive an indictment of the gulags as Solzhenitsyn's work was to be, except more economical, brisker:

'Soviet prisoners ... were nonetheless fascinated by people who had been imprisoned for actual due cause.

In a hard-labour camp for political prisoners, Ivan Grigoryevich had met an adolescent student named Borya Romashkin, who had been sentenced to ten years in prison because he had actually written leaflets accusing the state of persecuting innocent people, and he had really typed them out on a typewriter, and he himself had actually posted them at night on the walls of apartment buildings in Moscow. Borya had told Ivan Grigoryevich that during the course of his interrogation dozens of officials of the Ministry of State Security, among them several generals, had come to take a look at him. All were interested in this boy who had been arrested for due cause. In the camps Borya was even famous.'

Grossman died in 1964, with his last two books, as far as he knew, not just unpublished but unpublishable. The posthumous publication of *Life and Fate* is implicitly taken as his vindication, his triumph over the Soviet state, similar to the triumphs of other writers whose work has found its real readership after the author's death – Melville and *Moby-Dick*, say. It is tempting to claim that, on the basis that the novel eventually found readers, there has been an element of redemption for Grossman and his work. That is what one wishes for Grossman. I wonder, though. *Life and Fate* still seems to me to be a grossly under-read book. Its first edition had a reception that may have been muted by the criticisms of the book in its own introduction. (Chandler's first go at introducing *Life and Fate* to the world pointed out Grossman's occasional ponderousness, and the unfinished nature of the book. But then translators sometimes have a too close view of their author's flaws – David Magarshack's *The Devils* comes to mind.) The bad news about Stalin seemed to have come in already; the novel's news didn't seem to be new. In Russia, too, I get the sense that Grossman is revered but not read as much as he might be. There, the nature of the accommodations he made with the regime put some readers off, and his criticisms of Stalin's Russia in its moment of triumph are not totally welcome. The upshot is that *Life and Fate* has never quite had the global readership it deserves. Now, when people are so keen to read about the Second World War – on the basis, I suspect, that it was the last time we in the West felt comprehensively and unequivocally in the right – would be a good moment for that to change.

With grateful acknowledgements to the London Review of Books (www.lrb.co.uk).

Target Russia?

*George N. Lewis and
Theodore A. Postol*

*Russia perceives new US
anti-missile deployments in
Europe as, in part, aimed at
its own forces. The authors
examine the technological
basis of these concerns.
George N. Lewis has a Ph.D.
in experimental physics and
is associate director of the
Peace Studies Programme at
Cornell University. Theodore
A. Postol is professor of
science, technology and
national security at the
Massachusetts Institute of
Technology and a former
scientific adviser to the Chief
of Naval Operations.*

The Bush administration is proposing to deploy a missile defence that it claims would protect most of Europe and the continental United States against potential long-range ballistic missile attacks from Iran. The proposed system would have its major components at three sites. One unidentified site would host a radar in a forward position close to Iran to provide early-warning and cueing information.

That information would then be transferred to a large X-band radar, known as the European Midcourse Radar (EMR), designed to allow US defences to discriminate, track, and identify a target cluster. The European Midcourse Radar, planned for a site near Prague in the Czech Republic, would be built by upgrading and moving an existing X-band radar from the Pacific Missile Test Range at Kwajalein in the Marshall Islands. The other site, a farm of 10 missile interceptors, would be located in the north of Poland. According to statements made by the United States, this proposed deployment is not only 'optimal', thereby providing redundant protection of the continental United States and basic protection of European Nato allies against postulated future ballistic missile attacks from Iran, but also has absolutely no capabilities against Russian inter-continental ballistic missiles.

The Russian reaction to the proposed deployment has been sharply negative. President Vladimir Putin expressed alarm that 'the [nuclear] balance will be upset', and although the Russians have gone into little detail about how they arrived at their conclusions, US descriptions of talks with Russian officials indicate that the Kremlin perceives the US deployment to be at least in part aimed at Russia.

In order to understand Russian concerns, it is useful to examine how Russian military analysts might assess the capabilities of the proposed US system. They would assess both the initial technical capabilities of the US system and its potential capabilities as it matures. They would look twice at US decisions to site the system as the Pentagon intends and rightly conclude that the system might be designed to counter Russia's deterrent in addition to a nuclear attack from Iran.

Current and potential capabilities

The clearest high-level statement with regard to US missile defence programmes is National Security Presidential Directive 23 (NSPD-23), signed by President George W. Bush on 6 December 2002. The directive stated that the United States would begin to deploy missile defences in 2004 'as a starting point for fielding improved and expanded missile defences later'. NSPD-23 was preceded in January 2002 by a memorandum from Secretary of Defence Donald Rumsfeld. The Rumsfeld memo directs the Missile Defence Agency to develop defence systems by using whatever technology is 'available', even if the capabilities produced are limited relative to what the defence must ultimately be able to do.

The Rumsfeld mandate and NSPD-23 would make it clear to Russian analysts that anything they see now will surely be upgraded to something far more capable as US missile defense activities advance.

Russian analysts would surely know that the US missile defense could be readily defeated by very simple countermeasures, such as decoys that would look much like basketball-sized balloons. The analysts and their political leaders also would rightly ask why the Americans are doing this.

What is the US intent? How will Russia have to modernize its inter-continental ballistic missiles and attack plans to keep up with the constantly changing character of the defence and the uncertainties created by it? What are the political motivations for the relentless US efforts to build defences obviously aimed at Russia? What is the relationship of the US missile defence efforts to the constant push to expand Nato and encircle Russia with US bases?

Russian analysts examining the system would also conclude that, at some unforeseen future time, under highly unpredictable and very specialized conditions, the European defence might be able to engage many hundreds of targets, thereby, in conjunction with other US systems, threatening Russia's nuclear deterrent. Such possibilities, however remote they would seem, would certainly conjure up apocalyptic threats to Russia's national survival.

The source of these concerns would be basic scientific facts that could be used by the Department of Defence in the relentless and unpredictable modernization effort foretold by National Security Presidential Directive-23. The location of the radar in the Czech Republic and the interceptors in Poland, both close to European Russia, would make it possible, at least in principle, for the radar to track Russian inter-continental ballistic missiles very early after a launch and to guide interceptors against them. Although the radar currently proposed for deployment will not have the capability to track hundreds of targets at long ranges simultaneously and the number of interceptors in the initial deployment would be small, Russian analysts would expect that the capabilities of the radar and interceptors could be substantially improved at a later time.

In particular, the limits of the radar's abilities to track large numbers of targets simultaneously are determined by the antenna's effective size and average radiated power. The Pentagon could enhance both of these variables, boosting the system's capabilities.

Currently, the effective size and power of US X-band radar antennas are limited by the number of transmit/receive modules that are mounted in their faces. Initial plans call for the European Midcourse Radar antenna to have roughly 20,000 such transmit/receive modules thinly distributed over its 100- to 120-square-metre antenna face, each capable of radiating 2 to 3 watts of average power.

Yet, the maximum number of transmit/receive modules that could be placed on an antenna face of 120 square metres is well more than 300,000. Such a modernization would require the complete replacement and reconstruction of the antenna, but it would result in a vast increase in the number of targets that could simultaneously be engaged by the radar because the 'effective area' of the antenna is proportional to the number of transmit/receive modules. If the number of transmit/receive modules were to be increased by a factor of 16 to 17, then both the effective area of the antenna and the radiated power would increase by the same factor. The two factors combine to provide a nearly 300-fold ($17 \times 17 = 289$) increase in capability.

Currently, the ability to build X-band radars is limited by the rate at which transmit/receive modules are being manufactured. The modules are also expensive, currently about $1,000 each. The current limits on manufacturing, however, can be expected to change over time as techniques improve. In addition, as the missile defence programme moves forward, the manufacturing base for these modules might grow. Thus, Russia fears that the X-band radar could target 300 times more missiles when a mature capability becomes available.

Russian analysts would also be concerned that the United States might expand the number of interceptors in Poland to take advantage of such a European Midcourse Radar's prodigious abilities to guide numerous interceptors simultaneously. Indeed, unless one believes Iran will stop building long-range missiles once they get to ten, such an expansion must be expected. Once interceptor manufacturing facilities are operating, additional interceptors could be obtained by extending manufacturing runs, by expanding manufacturing facilities, or both. The primary obstacle to an expansion would be political: increasing the number of interceptors would require modifications to an existing agreement with Poland. If Poland is already hosting US interceptors, the biggest political obstacle would already have been overcome.

Threat to Russia's deterrent

The location of the radar in the Czech Republic and missile defence interceptors in Poland, close to European-based Russian inter-continental ballistic missile installations, would raise questions among Russian analysts about the potential threat to Russian ICBMs based in European Russia.

The ground-based interceptors in some ways resemble inter-continental ballistic missiles themselves. They are extremely large, two-stage ballistic missiles, weighing roughly 21,500 kilograms each, with the two stages derived from the Minuteman series of ICBMs. They boast the same diameter as the

Minuteman III's two upper stages and even use the same shroud. Indeed, if an interceptor were armed with a typical 1,100-kilogram Minuteman III payload of a missile bus and three nuclear warheads, it could carry that payload more than 6,000 kilometres. The interceptor would only have to carry a kill vehicle weighing 70 kilograms, allowing it to achieve a speed 40 per cent faster than an inter-continental ballistic missile on a trajectory from Russia to the United States and permitting the interceptor to catch a nuclear-armed Russian ICBM from behind.

Despite claims to the contrary, US interceptors launched from a Polish site could intercept the 18 to 25 Russian SS-25 inter-continental ballistic missiles based in Vypolzovo, roughly 340 kilometres north-west of Moscow. Furthermore, missiles launched from all of the other European-based Russian inter-continental ballistic missile fields would be much easier to engage. The 40 per cent faster speed of the defence interceptors relative to the ICBMs and the early-tracking information provided by the European Midcourse Radar in the Czech Republic would allow the defence system to engage essentially all Russian ICBMs launched against the continental United States from Russian sites west of the Urals. It is difficult to see why any well-informed Russian analyst would not find such a potential situation alarming.

It would also be clear to Russian analysts that the placement of the European Midcourse Radar and interceptor sites is not optimal for the defence of Europe. Under the current plan, part of Europe is not covered and must instead be covered by additional shorter-range defenses such as Theatre High Altitude Area Defence (THAAD) and Aegis. A European system covering more of Europe could provide greater redundancy by using these shorter-range ground- and sea-based systems as a second layer. Ground-based interceptors positioned in Turkey, Bulgaria, Romania, or Albania; Aegis sea-based interceptors; and a radar closer to Iran would be better positioned to defend Europe from an Iranian attack and would be too far from Russia to pose a threat to Russian inter-continental ballistic missiles. To a Russian analyst, the only obvious technical reason for choosing the Czech Republic for the European Midcourse Radar and Poland for interceptors would be to provide interceptors close to Russia that can be guided by the nearby EMR, making it possible for the European-based radar and interceptors to be added as a layer against Russia to the already developing US continental defence.

Concern about possible future US missile defence capabilities would be amplified by knowledge among Russian analysts that US Trident submarine-launched ballistic missiles (SLBMs), as well as US Minuteman III inter-continental ballistic missles, are each capable of destroying Russian silo-based ICBMs. Internal documents produced by high-level technical experts in the Soviet Union during the late 1980s[1] unambiguously show that Russian technical analysts had concluded that Russian silo-based missiles could be wiped out by then-existing US forces. Today's US submarine-launched ballistic missile and inter-continental ballistic missile forces are yet more capable and pose an even more overwhelming threat to Russian ICBMs. Russia has been reducing its arsenal of inter-continental ballistic missiles and converting those that remain to single warhead missiles, but an increasingly capable US defence will create strong incentives for the Russians to reverse this process. The concern of Russian military analysts would be that a future crisis between Russia and the United States might lead to US strikes on Russian inter-continental ballistic missiles followed by the use of a mature missile defence to reduce or eliminate the consequences of Russian efforts to retaliate.

Putin's alternative

Putin certainly would have been briefed by Russian analysts about their concerns. Plus, he could not have missed the remarks of Secretary of State Condoleezza Rice, who, while in Oslo in April 2007, described as 'ludicrous' Russian statements of concern about the potential threat to Russia from the US missile defence system. In late May 2007, during the Group of Eight conference in Europe, Putin surprised Bush by proposing that Russia would be willing to make the data from an early-warning radar in Azerbaijan available to the United States. One month later in a meeting at Kennebunkport, Maine, Putin significantly widened the scope of his proposal.

Putin offered to make available data from a second, much more modern Russian early-warning radar at Armavir, Russia. He also stated that Russia would not object to US missile defence interceptors being stationed in Iraq or Turkey or other appropriate southern European locations, nor to the United States using Aegis ship-based interceptors as part of a missile defence for Europe. He suggested that Russia would be willing to jointly man early-warning centres in Moscow and in Brussels. He also made it clear that Russia was willing to discuss further possible ways to address the impasse with the United States over the location of the X-band radar and interceptors.

His initial proposal mostly focused on Russia and the United States cooperatively monitoring and assessing the Iranian missile threat. His later additions and modifications make it unclear how far Putin might be willing to go with regard to a European missile defence in the future.

Placing missile defence radars and interceptors south and west of Russian inter-continental ballistic missiles would eliminate any potential future missile defence threat to Russian ICBMs from US interceptors based in Europe. Missile defence radars would not be able to observe and track Russian inter-continental ballistic missiles early after launch, and interceptors would be too far from Russian ICBMs to catch them after a launch.

Moreover, early-warning radars in Armavir and Azerbaijan would be a great benefit to a US missile defence and would achieve US goals of having such radars close to Iran. At such close ranges, the radar signals from targets would be very strong and the line-of-sight to targets would not be significantly obstructed by the curvature of the earth. They would be an ideal complement to a Forward Based X-band (FBX) radar in Turkey or Azerbaijan and interceptors placed in Turkey or other southern European locations.

The early-warning and X-band radars serve very different functions. Early-warning radars such as those in Azerbaijan and Armavir use an operating frequency (150 MHz) chosen to maximize the percentage of radar signal reflected by cone-shaped warheads. Such radars are not able to resolve details of a target much smaller than perhaps 10 to 15 metres. As such, while these radars could track warheads with sufficient accuracy to support homing of defence interceptors towards the general target cluster, they could not differentiate between numerous objects that are likely to be deployed by a long-range missile along with a warhead.

These limits could be addressed by placing an existing FBX radar at a site in Turkey or Azerbaijan. The United States has said that it will forward-deploy an FBX but has not stated where.

The operating frequency of X-band radars is about 70 times higher than that of the Russian early-warning radars. Because of this much higher operating frequency, X-band radars can resolve details of targets to within 0.2 to 0.3 metres. If an adversary takes no steps to disguise the warhead, this resolution is sufficient to identify warheads relative to other objects of comparable size. Because these radars would be relatively close to Iranian missile launch sites, they would detect targets early and receive relatively strong return signals, which is advantageous both for discrimination and tracking. Unlike the European Midcourse Radar, these radars have relatively small antennas that are nearly fully covered with modules and thus cannot readily be upgraded by orders of magnitude like the EMR.

Thus, one or two such forward-based X-band radars could play two important roles in defending Europe: first, to simply 'inspect' objects launched by ballistic missiles and initially identified by the early-warning radars in order to determine whether they are likely to be warheads, debris, or decoys and further determine their trajectory; and second, to provide early and highly accurate tracking information to the numerous other elements of the defence system.

The high-quality radar data could be coupled with US interceptors placed in Turkey or other southern European locations or at sea, which would be better positioned to intercept missiles launched towards southern and northern European targets, relative to interceptors sited in northern Poland. The availability of such early and high-quality radar tracking data from radars close to Iran would enhance the effectiveness of shorter-range missile defence interceptors in Turkey and on Aegis ships in the Mediterranean or Black Seas. Such a combination of longer- and shorter-range missile defence interceptors and timely warning and guidance information from nearby radars would make possible a more robust defence of all of Europe, including the southern regions not covered by the current proposal for the European midcourse system.

Clearly, Putin's proposals open the door to potentially fruitful discussions that would lead to a missile defence configuration that would be far more robust than the configuration currently proposed for Europe by the United States. More of Europe could be defended and the system would have more reliability and redundancy. The reconfigured defence would pose no plausible threat of contributing to a US continental defence aimed at Russian strategic inter-continental ballistic missiles.

Thus, from a purely technical point of view, Putin's proposal to Bush addresses both Russia's stated concerns about future threats to its security and US stated objectives to deploy missile defences that protect its European allies while posing no threat to Russia. Nevertheless, policymakers must be aware of the costs and benefits of these two narrow policy choices. A serious discussion is under way about whether and how we could move toward a world free of nuclear weapons.[2] Because missile defences and deterrent forces raise questions of national survival, activities in these areas create powerful inconsistencies in state behaviour.

The Russians are deeply upset and suspicious of what appears to be a lack of candour, understanding and realism with regard to US plans for missile defences. US political leaders relentlessly deny basic technical facts that show that the current US missile defence might well affect Russia. The result of this standoff is clear and predictable: a world with expanded nuclear forces on high alert aimed at compensating for defences, and defences that will be so fragile to simple or inadvertent countermeasures that they will, at very best, have little or no chance of working in combat.

Any consideration of the potential costs and benefits of future missile defence systems either for Europe or the continental United States that ignores these technical realities in favour of political ideology is simply an invitation to disaster.

Notes

1 Undated internal and untitled memo on mobile missiles from the archive of Vitalii Leonidovich Katayev at the Hoover Institution Archive, Stanford University. The memo states that 80 to 160 US targets could be attacked with remaining Russian ICBM warheads after a US strike on Russian land-based ICBMs.

2 See George P. Shultz et al., 'A World Free of Nuclear Weapons', *The Wall Street Journal*, 4 January 2007.

With grateful acknowledgements to the Arms Control Association (www.armscontrol.org).

Fighting for Trade Union freedom

Build peace not bombs - no new Trident

Bob Crow
General Secretary

John Leach
President

Nuclear Mendacity

An Antidote

Christopher Gifford

Christopher Gifford is a Chartered Engineer who worked as HM Inspector of Health and Safety in mining and quarrying for 25 years. His work involved enforcement of the Ionising Radiations Regulations and some joint activity with the Nuclear Installations Inspectorate on human factors in high risk industries following the Chernobyl disaster in 1986. He is the author of Nuclear Reactors: Do We Need More? *(Socialist Renewal £2). Here he reviews Helen Caldicott's authoritative and accessible study,* Nuclear Power Is Not the Answer *(New Press, $15.95).*

Helen Caldicott is an Australian paediatrician whose interest in nuclear reactors and the associated nuclear weapons clearly stems from her knowledge of the medical effects of radiation in human reproduction and disease. She founded the organisation Physicians for Social Responsibility. Her expertise is not confined to medicine. In the writing of seven books about nuclear technology and nuclear weapons she has studied uranium mining and the processing and enrichment of the mineral into reactor fuel and material for weapons. She was nominated for a Nobel Peace Prize by Linus Pauling, himself twice a Nobel Laureate. This account, all of it guided by industry specialists with ample references and end-notes, is mainly about the United States and Britain.

Caldicott describes in a readable way how reactors work and what dangerous materials are routinely released in the process and in nuclear accidents. Reprocessing is also described with the resulting proliferation of plutonium and atomic weapons. When she has described the present range of more than 30,000 nuclear weapons, many of them targeted and many of them hydrogen bombs, which can be 1,000 times more destructive than a Hiroshima type atomic bomb, she has an uncompromising word for the whole business. It is simply madness.

All of that is before the consequences of terrorist attacks on nuclear installations are considered. The possible consequences of foreseeable accidents and attacks have not been described to us by the regulators nor by the operators who are required by British and European law to tell us what plans have been made for our evacuation, transport, shelter and treatment.* It is easy to understand why. In the worst scenarios large parts of Britain become suddenly uninhabitable. Even diminutive

---

*The regulations dealing with foreseeable emergencies are the Radiation (Emergency Preparedness and Public Information) Regulations 2001 SI: 2971.

accounts of that would not fit alongside a policy of building more nuclear reactors to counter global warming.

The industry's history of claims that it is safe, economic, peaceful and now necessary is the history of its mendacity. During the third of our recent government energy reviews, the new leader of the opposition in the British Parliament declared that safety was no longer an issue and the grateful then Prime Minister, even with his better information about the vulnerability to terrorism, took no exception to that claim.

Nuclear waste is not stored safely in the United Kingdom, as our Department of Trade and Industry claimed a few years ago. No one who had read the reports of the Nuclear Installations Inspectorate could make such a statement. Nor is the amount of such waste in Britain 10,000 tonnes, as the DTI reported. That amount was soon to be contradicted by the government's Committee of Radioactive Waste Management (CoRWM). Helen Caldicott deals effectively with the worldwide question of waste. She begins with the 250 million tonnes in the United States alone of radioactive tailings, finely divided, largely untreated and currently being ingested by local populations. We can forget about what can be fitted into double-decker buses when we read her quoted estimate that all America's radioactive waste loaded into railroad cars would form a train longer than the Equator.

The book is most topical in the chapters on the costs of electricity generation in nuclear power stations, the claims for new designs of reactors, and the 'carbon free' process that we must have to counter global warming. The new designs are just designs; not yet built, certainly not tested, and not yet appraised by our regulators. On the economic costs of generation, Helen Caldicott describes the subsidies and waivers of insurance and waste management costs in the United States that make claims of economic operation false. Similar conclusions have been reached in the United Kingdom. To test the claim of economic generation in the UK we need only to know that in three recent government energy reviews, two contradictory and the other judged misleading and unlawful in the High Court, none quoted the current cost of nuclear electricity. It is a matter of commercial confidentiality for the private sector operator recently supported by £4bn of taxpayers' money.

In her examination of the carbon dioxide emissions in the nuclear industry, the author sounds more like an engineer than a doctor of medicine. It is indeed her first chapter. She compares the energy units involved in uranium mining and milling, in transport, in processing, in waste management and in construction with the transmission losses and the useful output of a nuclear power station, of necessity built miles away from large populations where waste heat might otherwise be used. Her broad conclusion is that nuclear power stations presently cause one third of the carbon dioxide emissions of gas fired power stations.

But that is not all. For the future much depends on the availability of high grade uranium ore bodies. When inevitably lower grade ore would have to be mined and crushed, we could arrive at a position of parity between nuclear and fossil fuelled electricity. The logistics are impressive. For a large reactor requiring 162 tonnes of natural uranium per year to be refined from an ore body with only 4 grams of uranium ore per tonne of hard rock (an unworkable low grade ore but it illustrates the point), 80 million tonnes of rock would have to be mined and crushed using 5.5 gigajoules of energy per ton of rock. The energy used in those processes is mainly diesel oil and the energy used would exceed the electrical energy generated by the power station by a factor of three. The authors quoted believe that parity between uranium fuelled and fossil fuelled generators would be reached when the ore concentration is about 0.01%.

In chapters on nuclear energy and nuclear weapons proliferation, any stranger to the subject, perhaps a young person soon to be a first time voter, is bound to be impressed and perhaps confused by the contradictory objectives of the International Atomic Energy Agency (IAEA), which exists to promote the development of atomic energy, and the signatories of the nuclear weapons Non-Proliferation Treaty. The United States in the 1980s was the first to encourage Iran to develop a nuclear power programme, including uranium enrichment facilities, but now we read of plans by the US Strategic Command to attack Iran to destroy the facilities nearing completion. Iran's development is not illegal, although there has been some concealment no doubt to preclude attacks by Iraq and Israel, but the IAEA director, Dr Mohamed ElBaradei, mindful of the past concealment, still reports that his inspectors find no evidence of work to produce a nuclear weapon.

Every enrichment facility is capable in time of producing uranium sufficiently enriched to make a uranium bomb, and every reactor produces in its spent fuel the transuranic element plutonium of which only a few kilograms is sufficient to make a plutonium bomb. The world inventory of weapons grade plutonium is likely soon to exceed 100 tonnes. Plutonium in spent fuel now exceeds 1,500 tonnes and, on proposed trends, by 2050 could exceed 20,000 tonnes. Russia currently assists Iran to build its first reactor. China has assisted Pakistan to produce weapons, and the United States has supported India in the development of weapons to 'contain China'. Political instability in Pakistan is such that a terrorist organisation could gain possession of a weapon.

Helen Caldicott explains that one millionth of a gram of plutonium is a carcinogenic dose capable of inducing a fatal lung cancer. From bomb tests, reactor accidents, legal and illegal discharges from reprocessing plants, and mismanagement, it is already ubiquitous in our environment and in the teeth of our children.

The claim that renewable energy sources are not sufficient to replace both nuclear and fossil fuels is one of the recurring claims made in support of nuclear industry expansion. Some 'green' defectors, such as Sir James Lovelock, even George Monbiot, have aided the industry in this without sufficient inquiry. Helen Caldicott quotes research findings that do not underestimate the magnitude of solar radiation, tidal energy, geothermal heat, and wind energy, among others. That we have done so little about developing renewable energy is something that our present government has to explain because we have been reminded since E F Schumacher's early writings that use of non-renewable sources leads inevitably to shortage and exhaustion.

The land between the Rockies and the Mississippi has been described as the Saudi Arabia of wind energy and, in energy terms, exceeds the equivalent of all of America's electricity. Not even a fifth of it need be harnessed, of course, because there are other sources and solutions such as solar energy, hydro-electricity, geothermal energy, biomass, the recovery of energy from waste, energy conservation, local generation and the use of waste heat from power stations. Photovoltaic solar panels on fifty square miles of land could also collect all the electricity the US needs. Helen Caldicott could have quoted similar findings in Europe where the Bosch company has identified 100 sites for tidal generators on the coast of Europe each capable of producing the electrical output of a nuclear power station.

Helen Caldicott is upbeat on what can be done, and is being done, in the United States at state government and local level. The federal government, like the UK government, remains committed to the bomb and its further development, to the weapons industry and to the nuclear lobby. Her book will help to change that commitment, perhaps into more timely action on climate change.

Trident's Nuclear Winter?

Philip Webber

In a recent letter[1] to the *Bulletin of the Atomic Scientists*, I raised the possibility – based on some detailed US climate research published in early 2007 – that the nuclear weapons complement of one UK Trident submarine could possibly trigger a 'nuclear winter'. This article expands that analysis, incorporating further research carried out over the last year on the climatic effects of nuclear war.

First, a bit of nuclear history. Back in the mid-1980s, one of the highest points of Cold War tensions, the world's nuclear arsenal stood at over 50,000 weapons[2] and it was very clear that if conflict between the superpowers did take place, any resulting nuclear war would be catastrophic. That view is now generally accepted, although for a good while the Thatcher Government did try to reassure us that we would have a much better chance of surviving a nuclear war if we could shelter under makeshift shelters constructed of tables and mind-boggling quantities of materials supposedly available in the home or garden!

Gradually, working with colleagues in Scientists Against Nuclear Arms (one of Scientists for Global Responsibility's predecessor organisations), we were able to construct a detailed case that even relatively 'modest' nuclear detonations – of the order of hundreds of megatonnes (MT) – over UK cities would cause horrific deaths, injuries and long-term radiation consequences resulting in tens of millions of casualties[3],[4].

Dr Webber is the Chairperson of Scientists for Global Responsibility. His many publications include London after the Bomb *and* Crisis over Cruise.

Box 1 – How big is a megatonne?

One megatonne (MT) is the explosive power of one million tons of TNT – an energy release of 10^{15} calories. The world's current nuclear weapons arsenals total more than 5,000MT, or a little under a tonne of high explosive for every person on the planet[5]. A 'typical' nuclear warhead – such as in the Trident system – is 100kT (0.1MT)[6], or eight times the explosive force of the bomb which devastated Hiroshima[7].

However, some suspected that the longer-term consequences might be even worse due to adverse effects upon the global climate, as a result of widespread fires injecting huge quantities of soot into the upper atmosphere. Climate models were in their infancy by today's standards, but their results were nevertheless chilling. They concluded that as few as several hundred nuclear weapons could trigger a 'nuclear winter' with nightmarish consequences. This realisation was a key factor in dwindling public confidence in, or acceptance of, nuclear weapons.

Three climate modelling studies – by two US research groups and one Russian – were especially important[8,9,10]. They showed that a full-scale nuclear war – some 1,000 nuclear warheads exploded over cities and fuel-laden targets such as oil refineries – would cause reductions in surface temperature, precipitation, and insolation (energy from sunlight at the Earth's surface) so large that the climatic consequences could be described as a 'nuclear winter'. The effect would last a year or more and lead to 'darkness at noon' and other severe climatic disturbances. The stratospheric ozone layer would be destroyed, resulting in a major increase in the dangerous ultra-violet radiation reaching ground level. There would be major extinctions of wildlife, and most people on the planet would be in danger of starvation. The political response to these calculations was intense, with some arguing that the results over-emphasised the likely effects. Some even coined the term 'nuclear autumn' to discredit the work[11].

Nuclear winter confirmed

In recent years, of course, attention has shifted from global cooling due to a nuclear conflict to global warming as a result of fossil fuel burning. Research on global warming and climate change has considerably expanded over the last 20

Box 2 – Calculating the climatic impacts of the firepower of one Trident submarine

(*References are given in the text*)

1 Trident warhead = 100kT
1 Hiroshima bomb = 12.5kT
i.e. Trident warhead is 8 times greater

Blast area of 1 Trident warhead = $8^{2/3}$x blast area of 1 Hiroshima bomb
i.e. Blast area of 1 Trident warhead = 4 x blast area of 1 Hiroshima bomb

1 Trident submarine carries 48 warheads (= 4.8MT)

Total blast area of Trident submarine's warheads = 4 x 48 = 192 Hiroshima bombs

100 Hiroshima bombs inject 5Tg of soot into atmosphere

Total soot injection due to Trident submarine's warheads:
Low estimate (linear scaling): 5 x 192/100 = 9.6Tg
High estimate (using Postol model): 4 x 5 x 192/100 = 38.4Tg

Interpolating from the simulations of Robock *et al* (2007), the resulting temperature drop would be 1.5-3ºC lasting approximately five years.

years and, together with huge improvements in computing power, this has led to major advances in climate modelling, greatly increasing our understanding of atmospheric and other key processes.

With these advances, the Canadian organisation Physicians for Global Survival (PGS), Scientists for Global Responsibility and others called for the research on the nuclear winter phenomenon to be updated[12]. In the last couple of years, this has been carried out, with several new studies having now been completed[13,14,15]. These use the latest climate models run over ten-year simulations and with detailed maps outputting average temperatures and rainfall, with more detailed studies for key crop growing regions. Three new scenarios have been published. These calculate the effects of 5,000MT, 1,300MT and 1.5MT (the latter equivalent to 100 x 15kT), resulting in 150Tg, 50Tg and 5Tg of sooty smoke respectively from fires (1Tg = 10^{12} grammes). Most disturbingly, all three simulations result in cooling effects that last not just a year or two, as in the earlier studies, but for *at least a decade*.

At the top end of the spectrum, the two higher scenarios strengthen the basic conclusion that a large-scale nuclear conflict would have devastating climatic consequences (see Figure 1). They would lead to an average global cooling of 3.5-8°C – a change as great as moving into an Ice Age. This maximum temperature drop would last three or four years, with a return to normal temperatures taking about another seven years. Geographical plots give more detailed estimates. In the United Kingdom, for example, the average temperature drop would be about 5°C during the initial period. The global average summer temperatures would drop by 20-30°C. In two key crop growing areas, Iowa and Ukraine, detailed simulations show temperatures below freezing for two years and a halving of the growing season respectively, with a drought due to 50-70% reduced rainfall. Continental cooling would decrease or eliminate the land-ocean temperature contrast in the

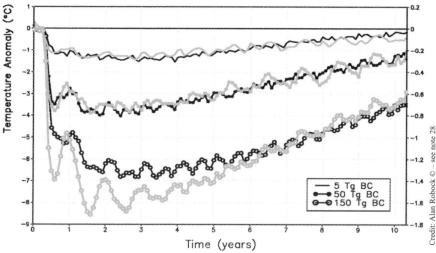

Time (years)

Figure 1 – Change of global average surface air temperature (grey lines), and precipitation (black lines) for the 5 Tg BC (black carbon emitted), 50 Tg BC and 150 Tg BC cases.

Credit: Alan Robock © – see note 28

summer and this would wipe out the Indian, African and North American monsoon seasons.

In 1983, the Scope study[16] estimated that the longer-term impacts upon the climate would mean that all survivors of nuclear attacks would have to depend upon food stocks for at least one year. Even assuming that the remaining food was distributed between survivors, the resulting casualty figures were extremely stark. Assuming no food production for one year and minimal food storage, deaths of approximately 90 per cent of global population were estimated. The only exceptions, in this scenario, were areas in latitudes 20-30° South, which includes Australia, New Zealand and parts of southern Africa and South America, where the nuclear winter effects were somewhat less severe and there could be up to 30 per cent survivors.

But the latest calculations mean that survivors would have to rely on stored food for several years, not one. Virtually all farming would cease for over two years, with a dramatically shorter growing season (if any) due to sharply-reduced rainfall for around a decade. To put this into perspective, grain stocks in 2006 were sufficient to feed the world for just 57 days[17]. To compound matters, there would also be major shortages of fertilisers, fuel for machinery, pesticides (but not pests), and seeds, coupled with periods of darkness during daytime, unpredictable frosts, widespread radioactivity and toxic chemicals, and a food distribution system in chaos.

It is hard to overstate the level of global catastrophe that this would represent.

These results alone need to be brought into the public eye as a shocking reminder of the sheer folly and longer term devastation that a major nuclear conflict would bring, not just to the attacker and the attacked, but to every country and region on the planet.

But if this is not shocking enough, research simulating the effects of a 'regional conflict' involving just 100 Hiroshima-sized nuclear weapons (1.5MT in total) concluded that even this could cause significant cooling for several years across the Northern Hemisphere.

Two of the studies mentioned above[18,19] investigated such a scenario. They estimated that such an attack – assumed to target city centres very rich in materials that would burn fiercely – would inject a total weight of smoke into the atmosphere of 5Tg. Their results showed a global cooling for ten years peaking at 1.3°C. This would still be a major climatic change, especially given the speed at which it would occur. Casualties from blast, fire and radiation due to the nuclear weapons are calculated to be up to a total of 20 million if 'super-cities' such as Delhi or Mumbai are included in the target list. The methodology to calculate these figures is very similar to that which we used in the book *London after the Bomb* in 1982.[20]

What could one nuclear-armed Trident submarine do?

After publication of the above results, I decided to estimate what the climatic effects might be using a small number of the larger weapons routinely deployed by the five 'official' nuclear powers. Here I take the example of a UK Trident submarine, carrying its full complement of nuclear weapons. The calculations are given in Box 2 with the explanation as follows.

One Trident submarine is capable of carrying 16 missiles with a total of 48 nuclear warheads, each one of which has a yield of 100kT and can be targeted on a separate city[21]. In order to estimate the climatic impact, we need to calculate how much black carbon (soot) each Trident warhead could send into the atmosphere. The amount of soot created for a given target is proportional to the area set on fire. Robock's 'regional conflict' scenario above used as its basis the firestorm that was witnessed at Hiroshima. Nuclear weapons effects are usually calculated on well known blast-effect scaling laws[22]. Blast damage radii scale as the cube root of the warhead size, thus blast areas scale as square of the cube root (i.e. to the power 2/3). Using the figures in Box 2, we can calculate that one Trident warhead has a blast devastation area four times as large as that in Hiroshima. Using the full complement that can be carried, one Trident submarine can therefore devastate an area 192 times that of Hiroshima. This is roughly twice the regional scenario – which assumed 100 Hiroshima sized bombs – and therefore results in twice the soot injected into the atmosphere. This also means roughly 40 million casualties if densely populated centres are targeted.

However, fire causation and spread is a complex issue and there is reason to believe the impacts could be greater. The Postol super-fire/firestorm spread model[23] predicts that for larger nuclear warheads such as those carried on Trident, fires are likely to rage over an area some 3.5-4 times larger than that estimated from simple scaling-up of the effects of Hiroshima. Taking this important factor into account, one UK Trident submarine could inject not 10Tg of soot into the atmosphere but possibly as much as 38Tg. Interpolating between the 5 and 50Tg scenarios, this magnitude of soot injection seems likely to produce a globally averaged cooling of some 1.5-3°C over at least five years and shortening of growing seasons by 10-30 days.

It is a shocking revelation that the firepower of just one Trident nuclear submarine could not only devastate 48 cities and cause tens of millions of direct casualties, but also cause a global cooling lasting several years and of a magnitude not seen since the last Ice Age. This would have a tremendous impact on global society and natural ecosystems.

More work is needed to assess in detail the impact that such a cooling would have. As noted above, food supply is particularly vulnerable, especially as world grain stocks currently stand at less than 60 days supply – their lowest level for over 30 years[24]. Helfand has estimated that 1 billion deaths could result from food shortages arising from the 'regional conflict' scenario above[25].

Implications for global and national nuclear policy

While the estimates in this article obviously need further analysis and refinement, they are nevertheless robust enough to have important policy implications.

Firstly, this analysis adds yet more weight to the argument that urgent progress is needed in global nuclear disarmament, through the Nuclear Non-Proliferation Treaty or, better, through a new nuclear weapons convention. With over 26,000 nuclear weapons still in existence[26], there really should not be any further delay in pursuing this.

Secondly, any nuclear arsenal over about 5MT (i.e. about 50 Trident warheads) should be considered a threat, not just to other states and peoples against which it may be targeted, but also globally through the climatic impacts that could be wrought. The five 'official' nuclear powers – United States, Russia, China, France and the United Kingdom – all have arsenals in excess of these levels. It is also possible that the nuclear arsenals of Israel, India and Pakistan each exceed this level[27]. Regional and national instability, such as currently exists in the Middle East or in Pakistan, should be regarded as a potential threat to global society, and the provision of support and resources for peaceful resolution should be given especially high priority.

Finally, this is yet another clear argument against United Kingdom plans for Trident replacement. Deploying a weapon capable of devastating the world's climate system is a grossly disproportionate, and perhaps even suicidal, response to uncertain future security concerns. It really is time to put an end to this programme.

This article was first published in the Scientists for Global Responsibility Newsletter, no 35 (Winter 2008) – Reprinted with permission.

Notes

1 Webber P. (2007). *Forecasting nuclear winter*. Bulletin of the Atomic Scientists, vol. 63, no. 5, pp. 5-8 (September/October). http://www.thebulletin.org/

2 Smith D. (2003). *The atlas of war and peace*. Earthscan.

3 Openshaw S., Steadman P., Greene O. (1983). *Doomsday: Britain after nuclear attack*. Blackwell Publishers.

4 Greene O., Rubin B., Turok N., Webber P., Wilkinson G. (1982). *London after the bomb: what a nuclear attack really means*. Oxford University Press.

5 The five 'official' nuclear weapons states currently hold approximately 26,000 nuclear warheads. These warheads vary greatly in size. The 5,000MT total figure is a conservative estimate. For further discussion, see e.g.: Kile S.N. (2007). *Nuclear arms control and non-proliferation*. Chapter 12 of: SIPRI (2007). SIPRI Yearbook 2007: Armaments, Disarmament and International Security. Oxford University Press/SIPRI. http://yearbook2007.sipri.org/

6 Butler N., Bromley M. (2001). *The UK Trident system in the 21st century*. Research Report 2001.3. British American Security Information Council (BASIC). http://www.basicint.org/pubs/Research/UKtrident.pdf

7 The Committee for the Compilation of Material on Damage Caused by the Atomic Bombs on Hiroshima and Nagasaki (1981). *Hiroshima and Nagasaki: the physical, medical and social effects of the atomic bombings*. Hutchinson. (Translation by Ishikawa E., Swain D.)

8 Crutzen P.J., Birks J.W. (1982). *The atmosphere after a nuclear war: twilight at noon*. Ambio, vol. 11, pp.115-125.

19 Aleksandrov V.V., Stenchikov G.L. (1983). *On the modelling of the climatic consequences of the nuclear war*. Proc Applied Math. Computing Centre, USSR Academy of Sciences, Moscow.

10 Turco R.P., Toon O.B., Ackerman T.P., Pollack J.B., Sagan C. (1984). *The climatic effects of nuclear war.* Scientific American, vol. 251, pp. 33-43 (August).

11 pp. 987-988 of: Thompson S.L., Schneider S.H. (1986). *Nuclear winter reappraised.* Foreign Affairs, vol. 64, pp. 981-1005 (summer).

12 Parkinson S. (2003). *Does anybody remember the nuclear winter?* SGR Newsletter. No. 27, pp. 6-7 (July). Scientists for Global Responsibility. http://www.sgr.org.uk/

13 Robock A., Oman L., Stenchikov G.L. (2007). *Nuclear winter revisited with a modern climate model and current nuclear arsenals: still catastrophic consequences.* Journal of Geophysical Research, vol. 112, no. D13, D13107.

14 Toon O.B., Turco R.P., Robock A., Bardeen C., Oman L., Stenchikov G.L. (2007). *Atmospheric effects and societal consequences of regional scale nuclear conflicts and acts of individual nuclear terrorism.* Atmospheric Chemistry and Physics, vol. 7, no. 8, pp. 1973-2002.

15 Robock A., Oman L., Stenchikov G.L., Toon O.B., Bardeen C., Turco R.P. (2007). *Climatic consequences of regional nuclear conflicts.* Atmospheric Chemistry and Physics, vol. 7, no. 8, pp. 2003-2012.

16 Turco R., Toon B., Ackerman T., Pollack J., Sagan S. (1983). *Nuclear winter: global consequences of multiple nuclear explosions.* Science, vol. 222, pp. 1283-1292. Further information can be found in: SCOPE ENUWAR Committee (1987). *Environmental consequences of nuclear war: an update – severe global-scale effects of nuclear war reaffirmed.* Environment, vol. 29, no. 4, pp. 4-5, 46.

17 Earth Policy Institute (2006). *Grain indicator data.* http://www.earth-policy.org/Indicators/Grain/2006_data.htm

18 As note 14

19 As note 15

20 As note 4

21 As note 6

22 Glasstone S., Dolan P.J. (eds.) (1980). *The effects of nuclear weapons.* US Dept. of Energy and US Dept. of Defense.

23 Postol T. (1986). *Possible fatalities from super-fires following nuclear attacks on or near urban areas.* Institute of Medicine. Published as an open book at: http://www.nap.edu/openbook.php?record_id=940&page=15

24 The low level of world grain stocks is due to a combination of numerous factors including soil erosion, population growth, growth in meat consumption and, recently, a large expansion in biofuel production.

25 Helfand I. (2007). *An assessment of the extent of projected global famine resulting from limited, regional nuclear war.* Conference paper presented at: Nuclear Weapons: The Final Pandemic – Preventing Proliferation and Achieving Abolition (London, October 3). http://www.ippnw.org/News/Reports/HelfandFaminePaper.pdf

26 As note 5

27 As note 5. See also p.18 of: Wolfsthal J. (2005). *Weapons around the world. Physics World.* August. http://physicsweb.org/

28 Robock (2007). *Climatic consequences of regional nuclear conflict.* Powerpoint presentation. http://climate.envsci.rutgers.edu/robock/NuclearWinterForDistribution 4.ppt.

Numerative

The New World Order recoils, recounts an abiding tale:
9/11 is text & pretext, 24/7.
U.S. crusades can't now be allowed to fail;
the twin powers, Might & Right, shall surely both prevail.
Great Leaders 'don't do numbers' – Discounting the foreign dead,
they assess 'collateral damage', smile white in each grey head.
Patriots duly multiply, regroup and seize the day;
they invoke their watch-word *History*, a parlous game to play.

Guilty parties pass unreckoned, none summoned to account
for torture or killing or mere doubledealing.
Fall guys fill the bill as death hangs around
and old scores are settled. Still, cashflow's appealing:
why crucify crooks who cook up their books?
Better to quote them, extol and promote them,
reward them, applaud them – new myths that astound!
Yet media mercenaries can't help revealing
just what neoconmanship's all about.

Propaganda, it's plain, should always work wonders,
excusing abuses, egregious blunders.
(Joe Public nods, passive.) Every trough needs its snout …
Words, money and guns politicians try stealing
to buy off rebellion, forestall left-wing squealing,
divide all dissent. Cabals rule the day,
pay head to no outcry. Allegations abound
which suit the State fixer right down to the ground:
commissions, inquiries, inquests, plus endless dull delay,
tell us *Truth* lies somewhere deep-buried, withered quite away.
Weight of numbers, statistics, are prime ploys for concealing
disfigured digits that add up to blank nothing.
But come countdown to Zero, there's no villain or hero:
all things being equal, the sums balance out.

Alexis Lykiard

TRIDENT is aimed at coercion, causes destruction and divides our world.

AID sets its sights on making friends, spreading peace and encouraging development.

Which is the civilized choice?

Keith Norman
General Secretary

Alan Donnelly
President

ASLEF the train drivers' union
www.aslef.org.uk

THE BERTRAND RUSSELL PEACE FOUNDATION
DOSSIER

2008   Number 27

WINTER SOLDIER

US Veterans marked the fifth anniversay of the invasion of Iraq by testifying at the 'Winter Soldier' hearings at the National Labor College in Silver Spring, Maryland, just outside Washington DC, from 13 to 16 March 2008. Iraqi Veterans Against the War documented the sessions online (www.ivaw.org), including a report for In These Times *(www.inthesetimes.com) by Jacob Wheeler, from which these excerpts are taken.*

'... Iraqi Veterans Against the War's Winter Soldier hearings, held just days before the five-year anniversary of the invasion of Iraq on March 19, were inspired by the original Vietnam Winter Soldier hearings, which took place in the relative obscurity of a Howard Johnson motel in Detroit in 1971. (The phrase, "Winter Soldier" comes from a 1776 Revolutionary War quote by Thomas Paine: "These are the times that try men's souls. The summer soldier and the sunshine patriot will, in this crisis, shrink from the service of his country; but he that stands it now deserves the love and thanks of man and woman.") The national media all but ignored those hearings, and the documentary *Winter Soldier*, produced by 18 filmmakers who attended, was left undistributed until Milestone Films picked it up in 2005 ...

IVAW was founded in July 2004 at the annual convention of Veterans for Peace in Boston to give voice to active-duty service people and veterans who oppose the war in Iraq but are under pressure to remain silent. IVAW calls for "the immediate withdrawal of all occupying forces in Iraq; reparations for the human and structural damages Iraq has suffered, and stopping the corporate pillaging of Iraq so that their people can control their own lives and future; and full benefits, adequate healthcare (including mental health) and other supports for returning service men and women."

The organization's goals are political in the sense that IVAW seeks to do what the Bush administration, anti-war activists and the Democrat-controlled Congress have been unwilling or unable to accomplish: end the war in Iraq. But the Winter Soldier hearings in Washington DC were as much a forum for individual testimonials and a therapeutic way to come clean with stories of unethical behaviour, and even war crimes ...

Jason Hurd, an Army National Guard medic who served in Baghdad in 2004-

05, said his unit regularly opened fire on civilians. After taking stray rounds from a nearby gunfight, a machine gunner fired 200 rounds into a nearby apartment building. "Things like that happened every day in Iraq," he said. "We reacted out of fear for our lives, and we reacted with total destruction."

"Over time, as the absurdity of war set in, individuals from my unit indiscriminately opened fire at vehicles driving down the wrong side of the road," Hurd continued. "People in my unit would later brag about it. I remember thinking how appalled I was that we were laughing at this, but that was the reality."

Vincent Emanuele, a rifleman during his second tour in Iraq in 2004, described facing no repercussions for shooting at cars or indiscriminately firing into towns, releasing prisoners out in the middle of the desert, punching, kicking and throwing softball-sized rocks at them. Emanuele says he saw decapitated corpses in the road and drove over them, as well as shooting men in the back of the head for allegedly planting Improvised Explosive Devices. "These are the consequences for sending young men and women into battle."

Sergio Kochergin described how the rules of engagement became more lenient as the war wore on and the casualties mounted. At first it was necessary to call the command post to report suspicious activity; later it was OK to "just take them out. … anyone digging close to the road, we had to take them out." Kochergin's roommate shot himself in the shower in Iraq. Kochergin himself later came close to doing the same once he returned home.

Jason Washburn, who served three tours with the Marines, described opening fire "on anything we saw in town". He recalled a woman carrying a huge bag walking toward his unit. They killed her with a grenade launcher. It turned out she had groceries in the bag. Washburn also reported that his unit carried shovels (which would implicate someone digging IEDs) and weapons to plant on a body in case they shot an innocent civilian. He testified that the practice was encouraged behind closed doors …'

THE COST OF TRIDENT AND NEW AIRCRAFT CARRIERS

In February 2007, Professor J Paul Dunne and Dr Samuel Perlo-Freeman of the University of the West of England published a report prepared for Greenpeace entitled 'The Opportunity Cost of Trident Replacement and the Aircraft Carriers'. We reprint here some excerpts about costs from the Executive Summary.

The United Kingdom Government has announced its intention to replace the UK's Trident … The Government are also planning to procure two new aircraft carriers, along with up to 150 F35 Joint Combat Aircraft, which represents a major increase in Britain's global power projection capability. These purchases will dominate defence spending. They represent a major escalation of the trend in the UK's post-Cold War defence posture towards aggressive power projection and pre-emptive strikes alongside the United States. It could lock Britain into a highly aggressive and militaristic course for decades to come ...

Using the Treasury's recommended real discount rate for evaluating future costs and benefits of 3.5 per cent gives a Net Present Value for a Trident replacement programme, including acquisition and operations/maintenance costs, of £40bn in 2006 prices. To get a better idea of the opportunity cost of Trident replacement, it is instructive to calculate an 'equivalent annual cost' associated with this Net Present Value figure; that is, how much would have to be spent over the service life of Trident replacement to generate the same Net Present Value? This allows us to consider what alternative spending could be afforded if Trident were not to be replaced.

Based on the Carriers and the aircraft beginning to enter service in 2014, and assuming that production expenditure peaks from around 2010, we calculate an estimated Net Present Value figure of around £17.75bn, and an Equivalent Annual Cost of around £1.1bn. Combining this with the cost of Trident gives a total Net Present Value of £48bn and an equivalent annual cost of around £5.3bn per annum.

The fact that the UK economy managed to weather this decline in defence spending without any particular economic problems and in fact saw relatively good economic performance, does suggest that there is no overall economic reason that Trident replacement and the carriers could not be cut from the budget. Model based studies provide further backing for the argument of no significant impact and suggest that, with military spending allocated to other forms of government expenditure, it is likely that economic performance would be improved.

If the two programmes were to be cancelled, or not initiated, the study suggests that savings of over £4.2 bn for every year of service life would be made for the Trident replacement and around £1.1bn for the carriers and accompanying aircraft. Using the total figure of £5.3bn for every year of the joint service life of those systems means that cancelling the programmes would allow the Government to:

a. Take one and a quarter pence off the basic rate of income tax
b. Pay the capital and running costs of around 200 new hospitals
c. Pay the capital and running costs of around 1,130 new secondary schools in moderate/high cost areas, with 1,000 pupils each
d. Pay £11 per week real increase in the basic state pension.

ALEX SALMOND – FAILED PLOT

The *Sunday Herald* has broken an extraordinary story about a failed plot between Sir Menzies Campbell and Gordon Brown to prevent Alex Salmond from taking office after the May elections in Scotland last year.

'Sir Ming Campbell last week spilled the beans on his and Gordon Brown's attempts to prevent the SNP taking office after the May election. Secret talks were held – over the

heads of their own Scottish Parties – about how to keep Alex Salmond's paws off the
£30 billion Scottish Executive budget. Brown wanted a new Liberal-Labour coalition to
seize power even if the SNP won, on the grounds that it would have a majority of seats
in Parliament.

It may have come as no surprise to learn that Gordon Brown tried to fix the result of
the Holyrood election. Do bears defecate in afforested areas? Nevertheless, it's rare in
politics to have conspiracy theories confirmed so soon after the event …

Meanwhile, Jack McConnell, the former First Minister, has emerged as an unlikely
home-rule hero for having had the bottle to stand up to Brown. For we also learned last
week that Brown wanted Labour MSPs to vote for "anyone but Salmond" for First
Minister, even if that installed a Tory or Lib Dem in Bute House. McConnell refused and
told Brown bluntly to get his tanks off his lawn.'

The *Sunday Herald* comments that this story suggests that Gordon Brown was
'Labour's own worst enemy in Scotland'. Certainly, he showed a very poor grasp
of the procedures which apply in a consensus dominated Parliament, in contrast to
one ruled by winner-takes-all conventions.

OBAMA ON NUCLEAR WEAPONS

*The Russell Foundation circulated for comment some of Barack Obama's remarks
about nuclear weapons. We reprint the Senator's remarks with the date they were
made, followed by some of the responses we received.*

2 March 2007 'The world must work to stop Iran's uranium enrichment
programme and prevent Iran from acquiring nuclear weapons. It is far too
dangerous to have nuclear weapons in the hands of a radical theocracy. And while
we should take no option, including military action, off the table, sustained and
aggressive diplomacy combined with tough sanctions should be our primary
means to prevent Iran from building nuclear weapons.'

23 April 2007 'Finally, if we want the world to de-emphasize the role of nuclear
weapons, the United States and Russia must lead by example. President Bush once
said the United States should remove as many weapons as possible from high-
alert, hair-trigger status – another unnecessary vestige of Cold War confrontation.
Six years later, President Bush has not acted on this promise. I will. We cannot and
should not accept the threat of accidental or unauthorized nuclear launch. We can
maintain a strong nuclear deterrent to protect our security without rushing to
produce a new generation of warheads.'

7 June 2007 'I will work to negotiate a verifiable global ban on the production
of new nuclear weapons material.'

2 August 2007 Responding to a question from the Associated Press about
whether there was any circumstance where he would be prepared or willing to use
nuclear weapons to defeat terrorism and al-Qaida leader Osama bin Laden: 'I
think it would be a profound mistake for us to use nuclear weapons in any

circumstance involving civilians. Let me scratch that. There's been no discussion of nuclear weapons. That's not on the table.'

16 August 2007 'As President, I will make it my priority to build bipartisan consensus behind ratification of the Comprehensive Test Ban Treaty. In the meantime, the least we can do is fully pay our contribution to the Preparatory Commission for the Comprehensive Nuclear-Test-Ban Treaty Organization.'

16 August 2007 'Before we consider developing new nuclear weapons we need to consider what the role of these weapons should be in our national security policy. As I said in my speech before the Chicago Council on Global Affairs, I believe the United States should lead the international effort to de-emphasize the role of nuclear weapons around the world. I also believe that our policy towards the Reliable Replacement Warhead (RRW) affects this leadership position. We can maintain a strong nuclear deterrent to protect our security without rushing to produce a new generation of warheads. I do not support a premature decision to produce the Reliable Replacement Warhead.

2 October 2007 'Here's what I'll say as President: America seeks a world in which there are no nuclear weapons. We will not pursue unilateral disarmament. As long as nuclear weapons exist, we'll retain a strong nuclear deterrent. But we'll keep our commitment under the Nuclear Non-Proliferation Treaty on the long road towards eliminating nuclear weapons. We'll work with Russia to take US and Russian ballistic missiles off hair-trigger alert, and to dramatically reduce the stockpiles of our nuclear weapons and material. We'll start by seeking a global ban on the production of fissile material for weapons. And we'll set a goal to expand the US-Russian ban on intermediate-range missiles so that the agreement is global.'

Comment by Kate Hudson, General Secretary, CND

Will the outcome of the US presidential race make a difference to prospects for nuclear abolition? For the first time in many years, I think the answer is: it might. Something is changing in US politics. How substantial that may be is uncertain, but potentially there is a shift which is more than just spin.

This was brought home to me in February, when CND had guests over from the United States for our Global Summit for a Nuclear Weapon-Free World. One of them – a Republican and longstanding senior advisor on nuclear weapons – told me his views on the election. 'I'm backing Obama', he said, 'They call us Obamicans'. As he explained it, a number of senior Republicans, who consider themselves to be 'Fordists', see Bush as an extremist whose Iraq war policy has been a disaster. They do not want more of the same, and so they are not supporting a Republican candidate. And they are supporting Obama, because they believe he can win, where Clinton cannot.

This is a real indication of the impact of Iraq on US politics. But what about nukes? In fact, nuclear weapons have been quite a feature in the current contest. There is a real interest in the issue – thanks in no small part to the work of the US anti-nuclear movement – and the internet is full of information about what the different candidates say on this question. This is given more significance because there seems to be a shift in wider US society away from nukes – as evidenced by the ongoing Kissinger-Shultz initiative, which strongly advocates new multilateral initiatives on nuclear disarmament.

On balance, it appears that Obama is more open to pursuing global abolition, reaffirming the NPT goal of disarmament, and frequently reiterating the need for it. Clinton's angle appears to be support for a reduction in 'emphasis' on nukes and for cutbacks, whilst preserving US nuclear superiority. Of course, it is no secret that what is said in election campaigns doesn't necessarily happen. But this is an important one, and worth taking note of.

Comment by Helen Clark, Prime Minister of New Zealand

Thank you for your letter of 7 January 2008 regarding US Presidential candidate Barack Obama's views on nuclear disarmament. As you will be aware, New Zealand is a staunch advocate of efforts aimed at achieving a world free of nuclear weapons. We are committed to the principles of the Nuclear Non-Proliferation Treaty (NPT) and work with like-minded countries, such as those in the New Agenda Coalition, to strengthen the Treaty.

Achieving progress towards the total abolition of nuclear weapons remains difficult in the current international security environment. For tangible progress to be made, buy-in from all stakeholders, particularly those states with nuclear weapons, is vital. We therefore welcome all expressions of support for measures that would contribute to a nuclear weapon free world.

Comment by Maj Britt Theorin,
formerly Sweden's Ambassador for Disarmament

On the question of de-alerting, the United States should take *all* nuclear weapons off alert, not as many as possible. Concerning new nuclear weapons, he is right that there is no need for new ones. He is vague on the Comprehensive Test Ban Treaty. As regards a global ban on the production of nuclear weapons material, why is it confined to 'new' nuclear weapons material. The ban should be on all nuclear weapons material.

Concerning the role of nuclear weapons, by signing the Nuclear Non-Proliferation Treaty, the United States has promised to work to get rid of all nuclear weapons. There is no need for new nuclear weapons. With respect to disarmament, how is he going to reach his goal of no nuclear weapons in the world? He should read the Canberra Commission Report on the Elimination of Nuclear Weapons (1996), and also the commitment given by the United States at the NPT review conference in 2000, which is embodied in the 13 point action programme for total nuclear disarmament.

Yes, it would be a profound mistake to use nuclear weapons in hunting Osama bin Laden. Concerning Iran, please see my paper 'A nuclear-weapons-free world is achievable' (*Spokesman 98*). Of course, military action against Iran should be taken off the table. Who can defend another fire in the Middle East?

Reviews

America's Dissident

Kai Bird and Martin J. Sherwin, *American Prometheus: The Triumph and Tragedy of J. Robert Oppenheimer*, Atlantic Books, 721 pages, hardback ISBN 9781843547044, £25

The publishers tell us that this, the first full-scale life of J. Robert Oppenheimer, has 'been twenty-five years in the making'. That is understandable, because it has made a ponderous volume, and embodies prodigious research. But some of those years have been eaten up by the publishers themselves. The original publication in the United States was dated 2005: but the British edition has been waiting until the beginning of 2008 before seeing the light of day. It must be said that the book was worth waiting for.

Like another famous dissident, Andrei Sakharov, Oppenheimer became celebrated as 'the father of the atomic bomb'. He was not, however, a proud father and his biographers liken him to Prometheus who stole fire from the heavens and gave it to men. Zeus did not approve of this, and directed that he be nailed to a rock on Mount Caucasus and perpetually devoured by eagles. Oppenheimer was devoured all right, but not by eagles. His numerous detractors have not grown in stature as the story of their criticisms has evolved.

Of course, Oppenheimer was vulnerable to criticism. Before he became the Director of the Manhattan Project which steamed away at the elaboration of the atomic bomb, he had not only been a most distinguished nuclear physicist, but also a figure of fun. The family was very wealthy, having made it big in the garment industry. They lived in a splendid apartment which was also home to an art collection which was the very byword for opulence: a clutch of Van Goghs, the odd Renoir, and a small peppering of other post-impressionist masters.

But the great wealth which surrounded the young Oppenheimer did not contribute to his popularity. Neither did his precocious cleverness. His peers often found him distinctly unpleasant, vain and distant. The unpleasantness is copiously documented by his biographers. But they have a great deal more to tell us about his scientific work, which developed very early, and took him into the company of Max Born at Göttingen and Niels Bohr. His genius was completely evident, but it did not stop the lesser mortals among whom he moved, from perceiving it as arrogance. He corrected his distinguished tutors without any consideration for their own sensitivities. Was his abrasive treatment of student colleagues partly explicable by a growing culture of anti-Semitism?

What is clear is that, after a committed disinterest in politics, the rise of Hitler began to transform his outlook. 'Beginning in late 1936', he told the inquisition which confronted him in 1954,

'I had a continuing smouldering fury about the treatment of Jews in Germany ... I began to understand how deeply political and economic events could affect men's lives. I began to feel the need to participate more fully in the life of the community.'

But it must have been difficult for an intellectual, however brilliant, separated from his fellows by the accident of considerable wealth, to relate to other American students. It was easier to relate to the American Communists, naïve, simplistic and at times generous. In the mid-thirties, his father passed him a copy of the Webbs' book on Soviet Communism, about which they first appended a subtitle which asked the question, was it 'a new civilisation?' Soon after, they removed the question mark. Oppenheimer was by no means the only victim of this ponderous scholarship, which, in Tom Paine's immortal words, pitied the plumage, but forgot the dying bird. He had previously read *Capital*, or so he claimed. He would have been better served with that as his guiding text.

Bird and Sherwin present us with a fascinating view of Oppenheimer's voyage through the American left. He gave money to the Communist Party, and helped raise $1,500 to send an ambulance to the Republican forces in Spain. All these good deeds were later to become the subject of ferocious enquiries by his tormentors, when it was realised that the genius who had given them the atomic bomb was also guilty of supporting so wide a variety of humane causes.

By the time of the 1940s, Oppenheimer's preoccupation with the evil deeds of Hitler had come to be shared by General Leslie Groves, and Secretary for War, Henry Stimson, who chose Oppenheimer to direct the pursuit of nuclear weapons at the Los Alamos laboratories. To his genius as a theoretical physicist he was very quickly to add a remarkable capacity as an organiser, and inspirer of collective effort. Much later, the McCarthyite pack at his heels, he was judged to be unfit to share nuclear secrets. But when the bomb was being developed, his were the secrets that everybody else was sharing.

Be that as it may, Oppenheimer seems to have shared in the ethos of the Los Alamos project, and been borne along by its commitment. He even advised the military on how to use the new bomb once it had been perfected, at which point it could be optimally detonated. By this time, many of his colleagues, less brilliant, no doubt, had decided that they did not approve of the use of the bomb against defenceless civilians, and that the most that they could accept would be the dropping of an exemplary demonstration bomb where all the lessons could be drawn without killing anyone.

That was not the American way. By the time Oppenheimer's dalliance with the left had come to the attention of Senator McCarthy, he was already tormenting himself with the moral responsibility for Hiroshima and Nagasaki. The FBI soon characterised him as a nervous wreck, and President Truman saw him as a cry-baby. There were many others who were to weep, but the tears of this brilliant man would perhaps weigh heavier in Heaven than those of all the rest of us.

Ken Coates

Global Turmoil

Leo Panitch and Colin Leys (editors), *Socialist Register 2008: Global Flashpoints*, Merlin Press, paperback ISBN9780850365870, £14.95

The *Socialist Register*, which has appeared annually since 1964, is devoted this year to a global survey of movements and ideas since the inauguration of the neoliberal counter-revolution – marked, at its high point, by the advent to power of Margaret Thatcher in Britain and Ronald Reagan in the USA – some thirty years ago. The survey is comprised of some twenty-two contributions by experts, with a preface by the editors, Leo Panitch and Colin Leys.

One of these, by Elmar Altvater of the Free University, Berlin, traces the roots of twentieth century neoliberal theory back to two right-wing economists, Friedrich von Hayek and Walter Eucken. They argued in the pre and post-Second World War periods that free market economics were the only possible basis for a free and democratic political order. State ownership and economic planning were incompatible with this. All planning systems followed 'the road to serfdom'.

Despite this, after the end of the War, Keynesian economics involving state intervention and planning were the conventional wisdom, until the breakdown of the Bretton Wood system of fixed exchange rates in 1973. Thereafter, neoliberal ideas and monetarism advanced by leaps and bounds until they came to dominate international institutions, government practice and even universities which had been the cradles of Keynesian thinking. Their final victory was marked by the fall of the people's democracies in Eastern Europe and of the Soviet Union, which was held to demonstrate that a free market economy was the only viable economy in the modern world.

The Survey conducted by the *Socialist Register 2008* recognises the magnitude of the setbacks suffered by the left in the face of the triumph of the worship of free market forces. Many progressive national and social movements have completely disappeared.

A new opposition to neoliberalism and associated western imperialism has developed none the less. However, the movements associated with this opposition are not necessarily progressive at all.

The two main flashpoints of the struggle at the present time are the Middle East and Latin America. In the former, fundamentalist Islamic movements have emerged which are characterised by negative and reactionary features. Asef Bayat of Leiden, in his contribution, states that Islamism may challenge imperialism but it does not promise the emancipation of the oppressed. He cites, for example, terrorism employed against unveiled women, non-Moslems and Christian Copts in Egypt, and Iranian President Ahmadinejad's anti-Israeli rhetoric extending to a denial of the holocaust. Other examples are quoted, along with the viewing of all westerners as 'non-believers'.

He points out the fact that the USA and other western nations have supported and used Islamic fundamentalism against secular nationalism and left-wing creeds in Afghanistan and elsewhere. He argues that the question for progressives is not merely to challenge imperialism, but also to work to achieve the emancipation of all on the basis of the universal ideals of justice, inclusion and human dignity.

In Eastern Europe, the struggle against neoliberal governments can take on a totally reactionary character. In a contribution on Hungary, G. M. Tamis, a former Hungarian MP, cites demonstrations against the Socialist/Liberal coalition led by Ferene Gyurcsany, a former secretary of the Communist Youth League and convert to free market economics, who confessed that his pre-election populist promises were lies. The opposition to him was led by the anti-Communist right with motorcyclists wearing Nazi and Arrow Cross flags. An authentic left has not surfaced, according to this author.

In Latin America, the other principal flashpoint of the struggle against neoliberalism, the situation is different. Here an anti-neoliberal tide has been generated by the poverty, unemployment and degradation suffered by the population and has brought to the fore a number of progressive leaders. Some of these have actually attained power in elections, although not all of these have stood up to the opposition mounted against them by vested interests. William Robinson of California, in his contribution, accuses Luis Ignacio da Silva (Lula) in Brazil; Lucio Gutierez, elected in 2002 in Ecuador; Daniel Ortega in Nicaragua; and Nestor Kirchner in Argentina of buckling under, to a greater or lesser extent. However, a committed anti-neoliberal bloc which includes Venezuela under Hugo Chávez, Bolivia under Evo Morales, and Ecuador under Rafael Correa, is driving ahead with radical and redistributive reforms. It is, however, too early to be sure about the outcome. This bloc has good relations with socialist Cuba, but is threatened by formidable opposition backed by the USA.

The editors of *Socialist Register 2008* believe that neoliberalism and imperialism are facing accumulating contradictions and argue that the New American Century project for a US world hegemony has run aground. This is the result of the inability of the US to impose its will in Iraq by force of arms. They also recognise that, despite this, neoliberal forces are immensely powerful and their economic momentum has not run out. The current economic crisis is, however, revealing their vulnerability.

The book provides a far reaching study of the world situation. It drives home the sheer injustice and irrationality of the global neoliberal system, which is totally incapable of safeguarding human rights and providing the basic material requirements for a huge under-privileged section of the human race. The enormous wealth of information amassed here serves to spur the reader on to strive the harder for radical change.

However, *Socialist Register 2008* offers no easy guide to the way forward. It recognises the need to find new and better ways of educating the electorate, gaining power and transforming the state, but has little to say about the means of achieving this. Gregory Albo of York University, Toronto, recognises the success of the ruling class in waging 'class struggle from above' to defeat, isolate, individualise and disorganise the Left and the working class movement. He calls for the development of 'new collective and democratic organisational capacities to overcome global neoliberalism' [p.361]. We all hope this can eventually be achieved. In the meantime this volume offers us invaluable food for thought. All socialists will benefit from the study of this wide ranging survey and should be sure to get hold of a copy for this purpose.

Stan Newens

Venezuela – Rekindling Hope

Gregory Wilpert, *Changing Venezuela by Taking Power*, Verso, 312 pages, hardback ISBN 9781844670710, £60.00, paperback ISBN 9781844675524, £16.99

One of the most significant breaks in the otherwise all-embracing neo-liberal miasma that envelops the globe must be the events in Venezuela over the last seven years. What is so remarkable is the intensity and breadth of the initiatives taking place, not just about the future of Venezuela but the umbilical relationship between Venezuela and the struggle for a 21st century socialism. Would it not be fitting that, on the continent that saw the first practical implementation of the neo-liberalist agenda, with the hellish economic experimentation of the Chicago School (in Chile after that other 11th of September), that the socio-economic practicalities of its demise should be discerned?

Wilpert gives a succinct description of the main political events and forces in play, with special attention paid to the character, significance and role of Chávez. He points out, given the propensity of the very poor not to vote at all, it was initially middle class support that clinched the election of 1998 for Chávez — a middle class impoverished by the combination of a 20-year slump in oil prices, from the early 1980s onwards, and neo-liberalist economic policies carried out by the political double act of *Acción Democraticá* and *Comité de Organización Política Electoral Independiente* (COPEI). The 1994 election of Rafael Caldera as President was the last throw of the dice for the old élite. With the failure of his strategy of IMF loans and accompanying 'structural adjustment' policies to return Venezuela to a degree of prosperity, the old élite's ability to manipulate the system was severely confined. Chávez seized the opportunity and, with his military rooted party, 'The Movement for the Fifth Republic' (MVR — more a hurried, cobbled-together electoral machine than a party), plus an alliance of various left-wing political parties, and even a smattering of élite support, romped to victory in the 1998 election.

The central core of the book is a detailed account and analysis of the policies and the progress of the Bolivarian revolution in the varying areas of constitutional, economic, social and foreign policy. These are chapters full of information and are evaluated in the light of Venezuelan history and culture, but also on the practicalities of trying to build a new kind of society. Chávez wanted to signify a new agenda, a participatory democratic agenda which rooted out the old powers of control. As Wilpert puts it, 'Chávez reformed not just the constitution, but Venezuela's entire polity'. In fact, we have a state which has been reformed, with added presidential powers, but with completely new sources of authority, the 'communal councils' and 'citizen assemblies', workers on the shop floor managing their industry, and even semi-official armed 'local self-defence units' in some of the *barrios*. With the perhaps unexpected sweep of Chávez's early legislative measures, the old ruling élite saw its grip on power lost at many different levels.

After the period of dislocation caused by the 2002 coup and the aftermath of the oil lockout, the Chávez administration was able to greatly improve the living standards of the poor. Surprisingly, on the other hand, the government had pursued, according to Wilpert, a fairly moderate social democratic, economic direction in its relations with private industry. The author brings clarity with detail to many of the social and economic policies of the government and notes both successes and failures. The number of initiatives discussed range over banking reform, micro credit, promoting cooperatives, worker-managed enterprises, endogenous sustainable development, the 're-nationalisation' and reform of the oil industry, tax reform, agricultural reform, and always with insightful comments on the battle for a new kind of participatory democratic economy, together with the empowerment of communities on questions such as education, housing, health, transport and communications.

The rest of the book is devoted, nearly 50 per cent in fact, to an extended discussion of the obstacles to and possibilities for the Venezuelan revolution, and attempts to define what Chávez means by 21st century socialism in the light of the apparent failure of state socialism, market socialism and social democracy. Wilpert as a libertarian socialist believes that in spite of the difficulties, participatory economics is the path towards a socialist Venezuela. His praise, criticism and potential guidance to the Venezuelan and global left is obviously informed by the work of Michael Albert (of Zed Net fame) and his book *Parecon — Life after Capitalism*. Wilpert is an American who lives and works in Venezuela, and runs www.venezuelanalysis.com, a mine of information and comment on the ongoing changes in the country. His book, as he admits, is in part a response to John Hollaway's *Changing the World without Taking Power*. In his response, Wilpert restates the case that taking state power, whatever its hazards, is an imperative for socialist advance, and he remains hopeful about developments in Venezuela, but certainly not starry-eyed.

Throughout the chapters analysing Venezuela's economy and society the author raises a number of critical themes and observations. In the final chapter, the criticisms are clarified and brought into context by linking them with both the internal and external obstacles facing the Bolivarian revolution and its impetus towards '21st century socialism'. There is not sufficient space to discuss the external obstacles, but obviously the United States, international capital and the old élite loom large. As to the internal obstacles, the most important, perhaps, are those related to the Chávisto movement itself. Firstly there is the continuation of the corruption endemic in the old regime, together with patronage and clientelism within the new administration and grassroots organisations; second is the top-down management style possibly aided by the military presence; and finally the problem of what Wilpert calls 'personalism', the centring of political struggle around the figure of Chávez and his adulation being reinforced by government propaganda. Wilpert sees these factors as holding back progress and detaching support, presumably, from the lower middle class, small trades people and waverers within the working class, but he does not make clear their socio-economic status. The failure of the recent referendum goes some way to supporting this thesis as the opposition core vote barely changed: it was the abstentions by Chávez supporters which increased. The more general criticisms stress the contradictions between authoritarian 'top-down management' administrative directives, the increase in presidential power to drive policy changes, and the many directives promoting initiatives to bring participatory democracy at the base, overlapping and failing to follow through, leading to confusion and resulting alienation. The detachment of the educated middle classes from the government has diminished the pool of expert labour available, and preferment has become based on political sympathy rather than expertise. The polarisation of opposition and the underpayment of some officials have undoubtedly led to the 'patronage-clientelism' problem becoming worse. This is complemented by an inadequate appeals machinery and the lack of proper inspection and overview by independent assessors, according to the author. There is machinery already in place to some extent through the Local Public Planning Councils and, as Wilpert states, 'the principle of social auditing is a key element in Venezuela's concept of participatory democracy'. This obviously needs to deepen as a process, which will take time.

For Wilpert there is also the question of Chávez's role. He is a man of undoubted charisma and considerable panache, a physically brave, knowledgeable and wily leader whose empathy with the oppressed of the *barrios* is beyond dispute. Given the Venezuelan, if not Latin American, culture of the *caudillo* or 'strongman' it is perhaps unsurprising that Chavez has to appear the 'big fixer', negotiating his way through the various factions in the alliance, and yet the author fears that government propaganda, whilst not manufacturing a personality cult, over-personalises political campaigning around the figure of Chávez. 'With Chávez everything, without Chávez nothing' is quoted by Wilpert as an exemplar. So much depends on Chávez that his assassination would trigger major problems for the movement; it could 'fall apart' without his unifying presence. Chávez is undoubtedly aware of many of these problems and the other major deformations of clientelism and patronage, which is why he has moved to form a mass political party, the United Socialist Party of Venezuela. Wilpert is hopeful that it will establish proper organised debates over policy, democratically chosen candidates for elected posts (not appointed by the party hierarchy, as at present), and above all a party responsive to its grassroots, which numbers initially a staggering 1.4

million. And, as Chávez says, 'a new party needs new faces', and the revolution 'cannot depend on one person or an élite, rather it must be based on the people'.

The book concludes its assessment of the progress, hopes and prospects of the Venezuela revolution in May 2007, so necessarily it does not touch on the defeated referendum, but more recent developments can be followed on www.venezuelanalysis.com. We can be certain, though, that despite the claims of such opinion formers as *The Economist (6/12/07)* that this is 'the beginning of the end for Hugo Chávez', the revolutionary process will deepen, not falter, if Chávez carries out his promise to 'revise, rectify and reimpulse'.

John Daniels

Why Nato?

Graham Hallett, *European Security in the Post-Soviet Age: The Case against Nato,* **302 pages, William Sessions Ltd, paperback ISBN 0781850723585, £7.99**

We know that the North Atlantic Treaty Organisation was formed after World War Two for the mutual defence of nations bordering the North Atlantic, but where is the enemy now, and are we in danger of mission creep? Afghanistan is a long way from the North Atlantic, and the author of this well researched and carefully written book believes that the 'War on Terror' is already in need of critical review, before we have more self-justifying, but unnecessary, killing fields like Iraq.

Graham Hallett is described on the back cover as a retired lecturer and a former Research Fellow of the Alexander von Humboldt Foundation. In this book he examines not only Nato's history but also, rather like Gore Vidal and Noam Chomsky, the foreign policy of the United States, particularly since 1949. In a table estimating the number of deaths attributable to America's wars since independence, his total for Americans, including those killed in Vietnam, exceeds one million; for America's allies and enemies and their civilians the total is many times larger. But nothing compares with the near 20 million lives lost up to and including World War Two in the territories that became the Soviet Union. The least accountable wars of intervention will remain those in Latin America, which deterred democracy for so long under the banner of anti-communism.

The author is not anti-American: like many of us, he finds much to admire in America, its constitution and its peoples. But in its military history, its foreign policy and its covert operations, he sees the need for greater scrutiny, if only to avoid anti-democratic activity and other errors being repeated.

Three central chapters deal with Europe, Nato and the break-up of the Yugoslav Federation. Was it reasonable, legal or necessary to employ 'carpet bombing', 'coercive bombing' and 'punitive bombing' to effect change in Yugoslavia? In 1999, eight of Belgrade's bridges were destroyed by Nato, and much pollution of the Danube was caused by attacks on other targets. In Kosovo, to avoid damage from ground-based weapons, bombers flew at 15,000 feet, and pilots were not able to distinguish between military or civilian convoys. One such civilian convoy was attacked and destroyed.

President Milosevic had understandably refused the terms of the original Rambouillet proposals, which would have allowed regime change, and given Nato forces indefinite access to every part of Yugoslavia with immunity from Yugoslav law. Notwithstanding the bombing, he continued to refuse to surrender.

Nato's objectives, authority and legitimacy are examined in close detail. Were the 26 members of Nato fully consulted on the use of 32,000 tons of bombs dropped on Yugoslavia and the capital city of a European state? Did they or the United Nations agree to the formation of the largest US military base outside America, Camp Bondsteel, in Kosovo, conveniently situated close to the route of a pipeline stretching from the Caspian to the Adriatic Sea? Did Nato's authority trump that of the United Nations?

Using sources as credible as the International Commission on Kosovo and the UK House of Commons Defence and Foreign Affairs Committees, the author is able to show that much of the information offered in support of 'humanitarian' interventions was unreliable. There was clearly some manipulation in Nato's US links with the Organisation for Security and Cooperation in Europe (OSCE), now a 55 member state organisation, which led to the formation of the Kosovo Verification Mission led by a maverick former US Ambassador, William Walker. He employed, among others, 150 US Dyncorp mercenaries who had fought with the Bosnian army against the Bosnian Serbs, and his car carried the flag of the United States. William Walker had claimed that Archbishop Romero was killed in San Salvador by insurgents wearing San Salvador army uniforms, and it is far from clear how his appointment could have been endorsed by the members of Nato or of the OSCE.

Fighting continued in Kosovo between the Kosovo Liberation Army (KLA) and forces of the Federal Republic of Yugoslav. It is not made clear who was supplying the KLA and encouraging its ceasefire violations, but the House of Commons Defence Committee is quoted as using language which endorses a 'widespread belief' that the United States was involved. A footnote refers to Noam Chomsky whose sources are usually incontrovertible, and a later reference aligns the International Commission with the notion that not enough action was being taken to constrain the KLA. The evidence for the anticipated 'genocide' used to justify the bombing seems not to have been found, although there were undoubted war crimes, expulsions of Kosovo Albanians, and war casualties of several thousands.

After several months of bombing, including 'Phase3' bombing of 'strategic civilian targets', the German Foreign Minister, Joschka Fischer, proposed a halt to allow negotiations. He was supported by Lord Healey, who suggested Russian involvement in negotiations rather than a 'gangster state' controlled by the KLA. By June 1999, Nato was facing the options of withdrawal, escalation of bombing to an 'all-out blitzkrieg', or a ground invasion. Large numbers of B52 bombers capable of 'carpet bombing' had been flown to bases in Britain.

As Lord Healey had hinted, it was Russian influence which brought the war to an end. A Swedish diplomat, Peter Kastenfeld, succeeded in obtaining Russia's backing for a set of proposals which made five important concessions, as compared with the earlier rejected Rambouillet proposals.

1 Kosovo would be under the control of a UN force (K-For) guided by General Assembly Resolution 1244.

2 Kosovo would remain part of Serbia.

3 Nato troops would not operate throughout Yugoslavia without being subject to Yugoslav law.

4 K-For would include Russian, British, French and American troops.

5 After their replacement by K-For, some units of the Yugoslav army would be allowed to return to protect holy places of the Serbian Orthodox Church and to prevent illegal immigration from Albania.

An agreement was signed on 9 June 1999. British General Sir Mike Jackson was put in command of K-For.

When Yugoslav army units had withdrawn from Kosovo, the United States reneged on sections 4 and 5 of the agreement and refused to accept a Russian role in K-For. In spite of the US requiring the Hungarian government to stop the planned movement of Russian troops through Hungary, a detachment was flown to Pristina Airport. General Wesley Clark, Supreme Allied Commander in Europe (SACEUR), threatened the 'accidental' shooting down of any Russian planes approaching via Romania and, on instructions from Washington, he ordered General Sir Mike Jackson to attack the Russians when they landed at Pristina and to prevent them leaving the airport. Jackson refused to obey saying that the Russian troops were under his command. Clark reminded him that he was the Supreme Allied Commander and Jackson replied 'Sir, I am not starting World War Three for you'. Jackson referred the order to London and it was countermanded by Washington.

Estimates of the cost of the war in Kosovo vary. The material cost of the air war and three years of peacekeeping is estimated at $97 billion; an estimate which does not include the cost of repairing or replacing buildings in Kosovo. Neither does the estimate include the cost of removing the contamination caused by exploding 30,000 depleted uranium shells – an activity refuted by Tony Blair but eventually conceded by Nato to UN inspectors.

Having provided much interesting detail of one of Nato's most recent interventions, the author goes on to examine larger questions of justification, authority, accountability, legality, success and failure, and criteria for future interventions, including those connected with the 'war on terror'. He discusses, first, the criteria for any war to be seen as a 'just' war, and concludes that 'humanitarian' wars must be founded on reliable evidence and not on hunches about who are the 'good guys' and who are the 'bad guys'. He then examines whether or not the Kosovo action succeeded as a humanitarian intervention, and he has such difficulty in finding in favour that the answer has to be summarised as a 'no'. Perhaps we are too committed to the notion of leadership, both political and military, with too little regard for the checks and balances needed in the United Kingdom to counter, for example, the misuse of the Royal Prerogative, or the pressures on a president facing impeachment because sperm had been found on a White House intern's dress. We need better procedures before authorising military action in wars of secession. Think only of Northern Ireland. It seems that in Kosovo too many of the initiatives were being taken with too little involvement of the members of both Nato and the OSCE.

The war on terror is where we are now and the author has few doubts that there is already much delusion involved. We do not know how to distinguish between the terrorist and the freedom fighter, and it would be wise to think about that first before using such an expression as 'war', which apparently no longer has to be declared or directed to a particular country.

All of this author's observations are timely and appropriate to the still developing UK-EU-USA-UN relationships. Indeed, it is time to ask, 'what is Nato for?'

Christopher Gifford

NHS concealment

Stewart Player and Colin Leys, *Confuse and Conceal: The NHS and Independent Sector Treatment Centres,* **Merlin Press, 128 pages, ISBN 9780850366099, £10.95**

This is an excellent and important book which should be widely read. It exposes how a succession of New Labour Health Ministers, advisers, senior civil servants and staff recruited from the private sector operated in the Department of Health to restructure the private health care sector with a network of Independent Sector Treatment Centres (ISTCs). Equally important, it chronicles the failure of scrutiny. The House of Commons Health Committee failed to investigate the real aims of the ISTC programme or to challenge the Department of Health when it refused to provide financial information.

The saga of the Independent Sector Treatment Centres is clearly set out in three parts. The first part explains the launch of the ISTC programme and the first wave contracting process, which led to nine private healthcare companies being allocated 1.3m procedures over five years. By June 2007 twenty-four Centres were operational although some in the second wave of the £5.6bn programme may not now proceed.

Independent Sector Treatment Centres were presented primarily as using resources in the private healthcare sector to shorten waiting lists for elective surgery and diagnostic tests and to introduce greater choice. But the underlying aim was also to empower the private sector and to develop an NHS market. At least a quarter of the work carried out by first-wave Centres was not additional work but 'transferred activity' which would otherwise have been carried out by the NHS.

Since the book was published, more evidence has emerged to support the Player and Leys analysis. Department of Health figures for Phase 1 Independent Sector Treatment Centres show that only four centres were working at 100% of the value of the contract and four had under 60% contract utilisation (end September 2007). Yet these Centres were given guaranteed contracts requiring the government to pay the full cost irrespective of how many patients are treated.

The second part examines the House of Commons Health Committee's investigation of Independent Sector Treatment Centres in 2006. This highlights many important issues, at least four with wider relevance.

Firstly, New Labour's public sector transformation strategy requires the mainstreaming of commissioning and the creation of contestable markets. The Independent Sector Treatment Centres programme highlights the sham of devolution and local control. Primary Care Trusts ostensibly contracted with ISTCs but the programme was centrally controlled. Democratic accountability has been virtually non-existent.

Secondly, the use of 'commercial confidentiality' to block disclosure of financial and performance information severely limits the degree of scrutiny. 'Commercial confidentiality' is widely used to limit the transparency of Public Private Partnerships and will become commonplace as commissioning leads to more outsourcing. So how can there be any meaningful 'community engagement' if the public, community organisations and trade unions are denied access to information on policies and performance?

Thirdly, it demonstrates that key performance indicators (KPIs), value for money and quality and contract monitoring will be marginalised by the market making activities and partnership with private health care companies. Most of the key performance indicators were process and not outcome indicators. It appears that there was never any attempt to assess the impact of the Independent Sector Treatment Centres programme other than the extent to which it contributed to the development of an NHS market.

Finally, the ISTC programme is classic 'partnership' in which public service principles and values are made subservient to commercial interests.

There is only one criticism of the book under review. The analysis of the development of the NHS market in Chapter 3 would have benefited from placing it in the context of what is happening across the public sector. Player and Leys do an excellent job in showing how Health Ministers and the Department of Health planned to marketise health care and the extent to which they will go to manipulate and conceal the real use of public assets and resources. Other government departments, local authorities and public bodies are undertaking similar market-making strategies in the rest of the public sector and welfare state. Sector studies, for example in health, education, housing and criminal justice play a key role in building an evidence base. However, there is an obligation to set each of these studies in the wider context so that common impacts can be identified, lessons learnt and alternative policies and strategies devised.

Those who believed that there would be a change of policy under Brown have been proved right – the drive to marketisation and privatisation has intensified! The words 'lies' and 'deceit' would be more accurate in the title of the book, reflecting the depths to which markets and neoliberal ideology drive political ambition and greed.

Dexter Whitfield

Official Lies

George Monbiot, *Bring on the Apocalypse: Six Arguments for Global Justice*, Atlantic Books for The Guardian, 242 pages, ISBN 9781843546566, £11.99

This is a selection of George Monbiot's *Guardian* articles published between 2003 and 2007. It is an invaluable source of evidence, with detailed references, for all the disputed issues – Saddam Hussein's Weapons of Mass Destruction, cluster bombs, arms sales, Palestine, religious fundamentalism, the use of torture, carbon dioxide emissions, extending airports, genetically modified crops, teenage pregnancies, private finance initiatives, taxing the rich, aiding the poor, health and safety at work, second homes, and much else. What is most striking in Monbiot's revelations is the extent to which the public have been told lies in these matters, deliberate lies, which were known to be lies – by the government, by the big corporations, by the press and media.

Everyone now knows that Blair lied about Saddam Hussein's weapons, that reports were not just 'sexed up' but rewritten to tell a different story which supported Government policy. Saddam Hussein is, moreover, generally claimed to have expelled the weapons inspectors, to have trained and armed Al Qaeda, and spread anthrax in the United States. And many newspapers went on carrying these stories when none of them was true. The Ministry of Defence lied in denying the use of white phosphorous fire bombs in Falluja. The employment of torture with prisoners of war and the British role in 'rendition' of prisoners to countries where torture is practised were all denied until the truth was leaked out. Rising carbon dioxide levels from motor transport, and most particularly from air transport, have been continually pooh-poohed in Government statements. As Claud Cockburn once wrote, 'Never believe anything until it has been officially denied'.

Many of the matters which Monbiot deals with are of desperate importance for human survival. The most serious is, of course, the threat of climate change from the rising levels of carbon dioxide. The trouble here is the mathematics. It is widely agreed by scientists that a rise of two degrees centigrade of global warming is the maximum permissible for stabilisation without major irreversible disaster for the planet. That implies a maximum of 450 parts per million of green house gases in the atmosphere, and this is the target which the British Government says it has set. But that is not true. The target includes only carbon dioxide and not any of the other greenhouse gases, especially those emitted by aeroplanes. The most recent scientific studies, moreover, suggest a lower target per head may be necessary as populations increase. Gordon Brown proposes raising the air passenger duty from £5 to £10 per head, which only reverses the cut he made in 2001. Meanwhile, airport capacity in the United Kingdom is to be doubled in the next decade, and believe it or not, aircraft emissions are not included in the Government's target. How are we supposed to trust what we are told, when such concealment of the true facts is taking place?

Reneging on promises can be seen as a form of lying. New Labour has a remarkable record in this respect. Government support for 'Make Poverty History', including speeches from Blair, Brown and Benn, promised reduction of debts and increased aid especially for the poorest African countries. This has simply not happened, and more aid has been tied to concessions to the big mining and oil corporations. Measures promised by Gordon Brown to control tax evasion by the super rich have not been introduced, and the gap in income and wealth between the rich and the poor is wider than under the Tories. Charges of corporate manslaughter, promised repeatedly by Blair himself, to bring to book the responsible directors of big companies, as in the case of rail disasters, have been repeatedly postponed and finally changed to a voluntary arrangement. The number of available hospital beds, which we were told would be increased, fell after 1997 by 12,500 in England and by 5,000 in Scotland. It is a sad story wherever Monbiot looks.

Don't read this book, if you want something to cheer you up.

Michael Barratt Brown

The Union's Scots Crisis

Christopher A. Whatley, Derek J. Patrick, *The Scots and the Union,* **Edinburgh University Press, 440 pages, hardback ISBN 9780748616855, £25.99**

As I sit down to write this review, the Scottish newspapers are full of the Union between Scotland and England. Our Scottish Government has already initiated a series of conversations from which it wishes to proceed to a multi-option referendum encompassing the status quo, enhanced powers for the Scottish Parliament, and the nationalists' goal of independence for Scotland. The aim of the conversations is to provide details of the three alternatives in order that the electorate can have an informed opinion on the subject.

Hard though Gordon Brown has tried, nowhere in these newspaper reports can I find the words 'British' or 'Britain' used. The term 'United Kingdom', as in 'UK government' appears because, on this same day, Jack Straw has laboured hard and produced a mouse of a report into the future constitution of that land we fondly refer to here as the 'Yookay'. But more on that later.

For, as if two initiatives on the same topic would normally be considered enough fare for any political day, the opposition in the Scottish Parliament has announced the belated formation of what they call a 'Commission' (Gordon Brown prefers the term 'review') to look into the working of devolution ten years after the Act to establish devolved government in Scotland.

The Commission has been set up by the Tories, Liberal Democrats and New Labour. It is embarrassing for the latter Party in that, after making the announcement earlier this year, they had to go to Westminster to get permission to do so. But now we have it. It can discuss anything but independence. Or, as the chairman, Sir Kenneth Calman, Chancellor of Glasgow University and former Chief Medical Officer, said at the Commission's launch, 'Independence is not relevant'. As in all good pantomimes, the audience of journalists couldn't resist participating, and a cry of 'OH, YES IT IS!' filled the room. Welcome to street politics, Scottish style, Sir Kenny. Was it ever thus?

The Scots and the Union is refreshing on this 300-year-old topic. Chris Whatley and a team of researchers have scoured the archives both official and of the great families of the period, a task of no small measure, to reveal a fresh take on the motivations of those playing the leading roles in this drama and how their judgement was affected by churches, monarchs (both here and across the water) and, of course, street politics.

Three hundred years on, the reports on these contemporary political events lead with the possibility that the Act of Settlement, which bans Catholics from becoming monarch, could be abolished. That this should be chosen as the lead issue must be perplexing to non-Scots looking on and, possibly, to indigenous Scots who have been ignoring the issue in the hope that it would go away. Why this issue, one may ask? Well, at the beginning of the 18th Century, the issue of succession was a make or break issue between Presbyterian Scotland and Episcopalian England on the one hand, and the popery of the Stuarts on the other. Scotland had just passed through what became known as the killing times when covenanter and Episcopalian were literally at each other's throat.

As for the Scottish economy, in an age of imperial rivalry and mercantilism, the lack of military and naval power hampered Scotland's colonialist adventures, a state of affairs that came to a head with the Darien disaster, in 1698, when an attempt to set up a Scottish trading post in Panama failed with the loss of the majority of Scotland's investment capital. Add to this three years of failed harvests, with an accompanying population decline of 13.5 per cent, and the scene is set for the lead up to the 1707 Treaty of Union.

Whatley spends some time establishing the shifting allegiances that lead to the successful vote on the Union on 1st May that year, arguing that the more common view that the parliamentarians were 'bought and sold for English gold', as expressed in Burns' song 'Such a parcel of rogues in a nation!', was not the whole story. Yet he does remind the reader of the amount of effort that went in to negotiating the 'Equivalence', the compensation given to the Scottish Establishment for its losses from Darien, and of the preparations of the Lords and gentry, with their bags packed, ready to dash to London as soon as the Treaty was signed so as to avoid missing out on the possibility of preferment under the new regime. So it goes.

The interwoven complexities within Scottish society which led up to that vote are covered in detail, but one has to be mindful of the sources for this study. Much of it is based on correspondence between the participants, the élite in Scottish society, but on occasions Whatley points to other elements whose ideas break through in to public cognisance. For instance, Whatley states that 'Union opposition had a plebeian character with Presbyterian ministers concerned with the attitudes of the poor'. This is further elaborated with the statement that the 'Covenanters introduced a radical, sometimes egalitarian and highly effective system of public finance' and that 'landowners should support the poor' with 'day to day relief in the hands of the church'. Radical grassroots thinking also emerged in Presbyterian tracts against the Union, calling for rejection of the monarchy, hereditary offices and most taxes, and the establishment of a commonwealth confirming a link between Scottish Presbyterianism and social levelling.

There is little doubt that the signing of the Treaty did not end the controversy of the relationship between Scotland and England. Open rebellions occurred in 1715 and 1745, with the attempts of the Stuarts to regain the throne. A further complexity in the web that was woven around the settlement is that Jacobites were found on both sides of the Union debate. However, their leader, without doubt, had his eyes firmly fixed on being king of a United Kingdom, and a plea of 'trust me', as a Stuart, to give you freedom of worship, seen by some as worthy of support, was rejected in the end at Culloden, which was not a battle between Scots and English, but between Jacobite Catholics and Redcoats whose make-up included many Scottish recruits, even from before the Union. Daniel Defoe, who operated as a Union spy, had earlier written that 'Scotland would do better selling goods rather than men's services in other armies, a sure sign of the supplier nation's poverty'.

(A digression: The National Trust of Scotland recently called for descendents of those who fought at Culloden to join in celebrations at the opening of a new visitors' centre. They could find Jacobites scattered worldwide but, try as they may, failed to find one person confessing to be Scottish Redcoat.)

To return to the issue of the Act of Settlement and why it should surface on day one of our contemporary debate on the Union, it was certainly a major element in the debates surrounding 1707. Accompanying this Act was the Act of Security, which made those accepting public office kneel before the altar. In Scotland this was seen as a popish posture; the presence of Bishops in the House of Lords as a condoning of prelacy. Is this relevant to today's debate? Perhaps it is, when our political leaders start to talk of oaths of citizenship and participate in oaths to the monarch. Lord Roxburghe, when asked at the time to comment on support for the Act of Union, is quoted as having said 'Trade with most, Hanover with some and ease and security with others'.

It was strange, indeed, to read the letters columns in the Scottish press on the day following the most recent contemporary announcements. All the old arguments surfaced, as if 300 years hadn't passed, which left me with the question why, since in 1707 secular ambition took precedence over religious rectitude, did we still carry that baggage with us? Our Leveller forbears lit a spark soon doused by church leaders in hock to the wealthy and powerful. How like our 21st century political élite. Surely it is time for us to establish a secular republic, or would that idea now, as then, be looked on as the crazed musings of a 'fanatick'?

Henry McCubbin

Popular Planning Now

Ken Coates (Editor), *The Right to Useful Work*, first published 1978, reprinted 2007, Spokesman, 288 pages, ISBN9780851247441, £12

Industrial relations, i.e. the ways in which immediate class struggles between capital and labour are envisaged by capitalist management, as well as institutionalised trade unions, constitute a very specific, and especially relevant, case of the old *problematique* of the ambiguous relation between grassroots movements and state power. On the one hand, as everybody knows, industrial relations, and most specifically relations on the shop-floor, still are, in many ways, out of reach of state power. Formally constituted as the 'private sphere' of capitalist employers, the entire process of capitalist exploitation seems to be difficult to access for political regulation: neither legal norms nor the 'monopoly of legitimate violence' seems to prevail in the ways that are claimed to be characteristic of the modern state. Even the Fordist system of corporatist political regulation has been limited to a kind of secondary access to the field: there are, in fact, tripartite processes of fixing rules regulating the legal and bargaining procedures concerning conflicts arising out of labour relations, but they do not seem to be able to shape those labour relations themselves. Take, for example, the historical 'normalization' of the working day: statutory regulation – as well as negotiated conventions between employers' organizations and trade unions – have not directly changed the situation on the shop-floor by defining the conditions of entering and leaving it. They have not even had a direct impact on the development of average effective working time. Their real impact lies in the development of effective wages, that is, by defining the proportion of normally paid working time to overtime.

Classical socialist thought has defined a perspective under which it was effectively possible to overcome this situation that is so structurally bound up with the basic relation of our economies and societies, the wage relation. That is by overcoming this wage-relation itself, in a process of socialist transition – thereby eliminating one of those uncontrollable antagonists, the capitalists, and making the other one, the workers, amenable to political control by organizing them into a self-regulating collective body. The capitalist answer to this classical socialist attempt has been the regulation of the labour movement, while maintaining the despotic liberty of capital to shape 'its own private sphere' – under different political forms, ranging from fascist compulsory regulation, via the 'New Deal' politics of trade union consent, to outright forms of democratic tripartism, as in the Austrian case.

The ecological crisis – as we gradually came to know it during the 1970s – has provided us with a new approach to the same problem. Controlling the ways of handling and transforming materials within the processes of primary production, secondary production (i.e. production involving productive consumption of produced goods) and mass consumption (with its characteristic locus, the private household, similarly 'out of bounds' for the controlling attempts of state power) has turned out to be the effective centrepiece of any conceivable strategy of ecological conversion. And this is just the other side of the same coin as the control of the effective conditions of work.

Among the early ecologists, most of them quite removed from the realm of industrial production, although far less so from the respective area of urban mass consumption, some consideration has been given to a seductive proposal of how to cope with the problem: to stop industrial, large scale production as a whole, and to go back to handicraft ways of producing (William Morris), far more amenable to political and social control than the ways of modern 'industrialism'. Less ambitious proposals have proposed a 'dualist' strategy: giving up any ambition of transforming those industrial production processes that turn out to be irreplaceable, and developing a 'second sector' of production on a more human, artisan scale, as the basis for an expanding 'convivial society'.

Both projects have one central flaw, aside from the questions of political realism they immediately provoke. They utterly neglect the very possibility of changing the concrete ways of industrial production by the active intervention of productive workers themselves (or of changing the ways of mass consumption by the active intervention of housewives as the foremost bearers of domestic production processes).

This is the very point addressed by the initiatives and debates on 'popular planning' that are documented and discussed in this volume which has aptly been re-printed now. In a historical moment when the Hayekian thesis that any political meddling with the economy is irrational, bound to lead to catastrophes and totalitarianism, it reminds us of three elementary facts.

One, that popular planning is not just another extension of the de-politicized administration management instances (and bureaucracies) are constantly trying to apply to the everyday class struggles at the point of (capitalist) production – it rather has to be understood as a co-ordinated effort from below to reclaim the equal liberty of each and every one to be heard and to be respected in their 'equal liberty', i.e. in the side-stepping and resisting all effects of established structures of domination.

Two, that popular planning cannot be restricted to the constituted 'public sphere' of the local or regional state, it has to extend, if it is in any way seriously aiming at its declared objectives, also to the 'private spheres' of the firm (*factory* or *office*), as well as of the household (in so far as they are still effective arenas of domination to be called into question by any real 'politics from below').

Three, that popular planning, in order to address the real needs of people, cannot restrict itself to improving the capitalist rationality of good use value for a good price, that is, of satisfying needs in the cheapest available way. It rather has to address the deeper questions of sustainability and sufficiency, by raising the issues of ecological acceptability and social usefulness alongside the question of economic feasibility and efficiency.

The very energy and dynamics of liberation struggles within production and consumption may thereby transform themselves into a source for broadening the scope and support for an emancipatory type of popular planning – by taking on board not only the narrow perspectives of capitalist accumulation and the individual reproduction of labour power as the commodity in the hands of the workforce, but also the broader perspective of real human beings living within historical political ecologies that relate to the terrestrial bio-sphere and embedded in a gendered cultural (and biological) reproduction process of their very lives. As the domination of the capitalist mode of production does not allow this to happen, struggling for such an inclusive way of popular planning means fighting against this domination – and in the degree to which such struggles succeed in reaching out to capitalist production processes, they begin to present a major challenge to this domination.

Such a perspective as that embodied by the authors of this book – before the neo-liberal counter-revolution seemingly swept them away – would today certainly involve a major conflict of powers within society. But such a conception of transformatory popular planning at the points of investment, production, and consumption – the determined way of life under the criteria of ecology, feminism and anti-racism – would not presuppose a seizure of power, as in traditional socialist strategy, with the implied amount of statism. 'Empowering the powerless' would necessarily be one of the central aims, and hopefully, also, of the central effects, of the whole process. But it would not constitute its utopian starting precondition. Which means that we can start with it again here and now, wherever we stand.

Frieder Otto Wolf

Artery Poet

Bob Dixon, *Make Capitalism History: Poems and Other Communications,* **Artery Publications, 116 pages, ISBN 9780953396511, £4.50**

It is sometimes said that 'you shouldn't judge a book by its cover', but here is an exception to that rule. The striking red, white and black jacket of *Make Capitalism History: Poems and Other Communications* by Bob Dixon immediately grabbed my attention and made me want to read it. Once inside, I was not to be disappointed. This is a collection of thought-provoking anarchist poetry and prose that will capture the imagination of anyone who likes to think outside the 'Capitalist' box. It is thoroughly appealing from cover to cover.

Abi Rhodes

Available from Artery Publications, 38 Pembroke Road, Bromley, Kent, BR1 2RU, (price £5.25, postage included, cheques payable to R. T. Dixon)

Space for Peace

Bruce K. Gagnon, *Come Together Right Now: Organising Stories from a Fading Empire*, Just Write Books, 248 pages, ISBN 097665335451795, $17.95

Since he got out of the US Air Force, in 1974, Bruce Gagnon has wanted 'to serve in a way I promised myself I would' whilst in there. He subsequently worked with the United Farm Workers' Union, which taught him how to organise. Active in the peace movement in Florida during the 1980s and 1990s, he became increasingly aware of the United States' plans 'to move the arms race into the heavens'. In 1992, the Global Network Against Weapons and Nuclear Power in Space was formed. Bruce became the public face of the Global Network and, since 1999, has been on the road 'to help create a global constituency to protect space from becoming the next battleground'.

These are the stories of his travels, throughout the United States as well as in Europe, Australia and more widely. In October 2002, Bruce Gagnon came to the Global Network's stronghold of Yorkshire during Keep Space For Peace Week, an annual event sponsored by the Network. Yorkshire CND pulled out all the stops, and Leeds University was packed to hear the two Bruces (B. Kent also in attendance). Since that time, the United Kingdom's role in US planning for star wars has grown appreciably, centred on the installations at Fylingdales and Menwith Hill in North Yorkshire. Tony Blair even offered to host US interceptor missiles there. But President Bush has found locations closer to the Russian nuclear forces, which are the real target of these emplacements.

Nevertheless, Yorkshire is the home to key elements of the star wars architecture. It is therefore fitting that the Global Network's website (www.space4peace.org) is hosted from there by Dave Webb, who has spelt out the actual role of these installations to readers of *The Spokesman* (see no. 70). That website and this book tell us much about what is really happening in our world.

Tony Simpson

unite
theUNION

London & Eastern
Region
Woodberry
218 Green Lanes
London
N4 2HB

Marking 50 years of CND

Let's work to ensure that we do not
have to wait another 50 years to free
the world of the madness of nuclear
weapons

On this anniversary, we remember
with pride the work of our former
Regional Secretary, Ron Todd

Steve Hart   *Regional Secretary*

020.8800.4281   www.unitetheunion.com

Demand equal rights for agency workers

NO UNDERCUTTING NO ABUSE EQUAL RIGHTS FOR AGENCY WORKERS

BACK THE BILL

unite
the**UNION**

British employment law fails to protect the country's 1.4 million agency workers. The Temporary and Agency Workers bill would outlaw discrimination against agency workers and is backed by Unite, other unions and the TUC.

On 22nd February, 157 MPs backed the bill, a momentous vote to end undercutting and abuse. But with government yet to back the bill, the fight for workplace justice has not yet been won. Keep pledging your support.

Find out more on how you can get involved in the campaign at

**www.tgwu.org.uk
www.unitetheunion.org.uk**

DEREK SIMPSON AND TONY WOODLEY

Joint General Secretaries

T&G section